FURTHER
SHEPHERD'S YARNS

True Tales to Make You Think

by
JENNY SPARKS

Illustrated by
Rebecca Johnson

MOORLEY'S Print & Publishing

British Library Cataloguing in Publication Data.
A catalogue record for this book is available
from the British Library.

Illustrations by
Rebecca Johnson

MOORLEY'S Print & Publishing
23 Park Rd., Ilkeston, Derbys DE7 5DA
Tel/Fax: (0115) 932 0643
ISBN 0 86071 520 5

PREFACE

Steel Sparks, my shadow and beloved companion in all I do, has sat, stayed and waited at my feet while I've written these yarns. He very much hopes his patience will be rewarded as they give you paws for thought.

CONTENTS

STEEL

On this farm the wolf actually does dwell with the lamb (Isaiah 11.6), indeed the pair have even slept together in the same bed. This is because Steel Sparks (my large German Shepherd Dog) is so similar in looks to his wild 'cousins' that my chickens cried "It's the wolf!" on their first sighting of him and that was when he was only a pup of 10 weeks! Now, at 3 years old he's just part of the furniture as far as they're concerned and he's walked underneath, grumbled at when he's in the way and generally treated with contempt. However, the sheep are still wary of him, when he will dash about playing 'stick' in their midst. But basically they regard him as a mutt. The cows ignore him unless they think he's posing a threat to their calves; then he has to watch out. The cats love him and affectionately rub themselves against him in greetings.

He, for his part, wouldn't dream of harming any farm inhabitant because he has grown up amongst this menagerie and quickly learnt that I disapproved of any attempts at chicken chasing or sheep harassment. By the time he was 6 months old, lambing had begun and the odd (sometimes very odd) weakly baby started coming indoors. These fascinated him and he liked and loved them, willing me to save them. He used to stare at the lamb, then at me, while I was giving it emergency first aid, as if saying: "For goodness sake help him Mummo!" (the name Steel knows me by!)

One evening during that winter the farm's main fuses blew on the transformer and he was left babysitting a triplet lamb while I directed the Electricity Board's repair man to the trouble spot. He and I struggled out into the blizzard while Steel and the infant kept the Rayburn warm. After about half an hour the work was finished and the power was back on and I was back indoors. But my joy at being in the light and warmth was short-lived. "Where is Lamb?" I asked Steel, as I began to search for him. I only needed to concentrate on the kitchen and dining room, as all the other doors were shut. But despite a frantic combing of this area, Lamb was nowhere to be seen.

Then an awful thought struck me, Lamb was very small – a few days old and about 6lbs in weight. A nice little snack for a half-grown German Shepherd Dog who himself weighed over 50lbs! Was he licking his lips? I began to thunder threats at him to see if he would look guilty: nothing! No response. At that point I made out a scuffling sound coming from my gas stove. And there was Lamb, jammed underneath it and stuck. Poor Steel wasn't in the least to blame and I had badly misjudged him. Now he is twice the size, it would be even easier to imagine such a thing happening but I know I can trust him implicitly.

This proved to be the case once I had the orphan kittens to rear. They were so minute they could sit in the palms of my hands and as there were four tiny mites, he kept losing track of them. If he was busy sniffing two, the others often got under his hind feet. Although his great weight on those huge paws would have been more than enough to flatten them, he was so careful how he moved.

As far as I am concerned he is my constant companion and I love him dearly although he's rather a chump. His greatest delight is catching and shaking his various squeakies and he'd like to play from dawn to dusk. He also loves a cuddle, but this is rather overwhelming when he tries climbing on my lap. He's actually capsized us on these occasions when the chair has been unable to stand the strain. Despite his matiness I often feel like Little Red Riding Hood when he's sat beside me. "What big teeth you've got." "All the better to eat you with." "What big ears you've got" and so on. And then I'm very thankful he's on my side and I'm going to make sure he keeps that way.

Those fine upstanding ears I mentioned, never miss a thing – they can hear a pin drop in a Force 10 gale. And so the night the thieves turned up again they never stood a chance. They had come back eight months after stealing a virtually brand-new 2 ton road trailer which I need to use all winter for the transportation of cattle feed. This is a pattern often repeated by criminals who expect their victim to replace the item ready for them to have another go. I was a complete flop, because I had refurbished an old livestock trailer instead and no-one in their right mind would want to pinch that!

Why didn't Steel stop the first theft? Well, he was only 4 months old and this they must have known, together with the fact that I had recently had my bitch German Shepherd Dog put to sleep. They must have watched me for some days and waited until the trailer was virtually empty (I was to go for 2 tons of roots the next morning) and they'd also chosen a very windy evening.

Steel and I were across the lane indoors listening to music which I was playing rather loudly to drown the roar of the gale. Perhaps it is as well I heard nothing, because otherwise I would have been worried that the cattle or sheep (both in their buildings) were at risk and I would certainly have gone out. Then little Steel would have followed and the pair of us could have been run down.

But back to the return visit. It was exactly 4.44am by my bedside clock, when I awoke one drizzly December morning. (The thieves were obviously in need of a Christmas Box.) Finding my hottie a coldie, I tossed it out, loudly clouting the central heating pipes as I did so. Immediately Steel barked and I thought "Oh dear, I've woken him up." But then a light shone on the wall over my bed. The only way this is possible, is if a vehicle is on one of my farm tracks. There was someone about as Steel knew, of course. I jumped out of bed and went to the landing window which has a good view of the lane and house gates. I kept in the dark so as to see out clearly and there was a car passing by and slowly going up the road. It then stopped in one of the farm gateways. Its lights went off, except for the reversing ones because it began to slip back down to us again.

"Right! That does it!" I thought, and rushed downstairs. Still not putting any light on, I let Steel out and he set off the security light and also had a couple of barks. Then, as all was silent he stopped to listen. The car must have been very near the gates, but was hidden by hedges. Then the thieves must have made a noise - although I heard nothing – Steel perhaps heard their voices or a gear lever shifted. Whatever it was made him explode into a frenzy of roaring barking. He rushed to the corner of the garden fencing and must have been in their full view. He looked like a Hound of the Baskervilles as he leaped up and down with all his fur stuck out.

So, without further ado, the car shot off, very, very fast with no lights on. A powerful and probably stolen vehicle. From my vantage point back on the landing (which gives a view east and west for nearly a mile) I could see that no headlights were used in the getaway. Those criminals knew their way, because at the top of my lane there are three choices of route (none signposted, just in case we're invaded of course).

While I had stayed bravely in the house, Steel had done all that was necessary and if you saw him you would know why no burglar would want to face him. He lived up to his name which I'd deliberately chosen, knowing he would need nerves of steel around here. Mainly to cope with all the farm's dramas and crises, but also to tackle intruders and all the while remaining unfazed by sharing his life with me (probably the severest trial!) I trust him with my life, and he is far better than any burglar alarm because he is a living security system unaffected by power cuts, the weather, or whatever. He never sees himself as off-duty and like all dogs he is a very light sleeper. He is the best watchman I can think of and that is his commission. And rather like Ezekiel, who was made God's Watchman to Israel, he must give me warnings, even if I don't like them (especially in the early hours of a morning). Then it's up to me to heed them and take action. Steel would never dream of not fulfilling his mission and nor must we as Christians. We are all (not just the Vicar or whoever) called to be witnesses (Acts 1.8), of his Gospel and of His Coming Judgement Day. We have a wonderful message of hope and one of dire warning, and both need proclaiming in balance. This is exactly what Ezekiel was told to do as we can read in Ezekiel 3.17-21.

Steel's continual state of watchfulness is so important as we never know when thieves may turn up – day or night. For example they made another appearance, one Sunday morning, when I was at Church (the only commitment which takes me away from the farm regularly). They stole a 12ft by 5ft high metal field gate, requiring a pick-up to transport it. Such audacity has meant that the replacement has had to be welded on to the hinges! Steel, by the way, was out with me that day.

In Peter's second Epistle Chapter 3.10, we read "the Day of the Lord will come as a thief in the night" (maybe even at 4.44am!), so like Steel we need to be always on the alert. We don't know when He may call us personally Home, or come for the whole world to see. So Jesus urged us to keep watch (Matthew 24.42) because just when we are least ready could be the day, as we read in verse 44.

Now Steel would never let himself be distracted from his guard post – not even his dinner is important if he hears someone about. He's always ready to do his job knowing that pleases me too. Is that how we are in God's sight? We wouldn't want to be caught napping any more than Steel would, surely?

X-RAY VISION

Visitors to the farm can be forgiven for letting their eyes totally deceive them. For when they come face to face with my cattle they quite literally see all creatures great and small, since the herd is made up of such a mixture of breeds. They usually  take one look and instinctively gravitate towards the smaller members – calves, of course, who disappointingly scamper off as they are not yet very tame. The smaller cows are also bravely approached, the likes of Gertie, Minnie, Nicky, Red (a deceptively small BULL!) – all now sold and Mispickel and April. Everyone named is a Dexter – a rare breed and the smallest cattle in the Western World. Some Dexters are miniatures, standing less than 30" high and weighing only a few cwts. They are very appealing and people often wonder if they have yet to grow up.

The great hulking cows like Isla, Honey and Folly are so awe-inspiring that if you are not a Cowophile you naturally shy away from them. The difference in size between say a Minnie and a Folly (a Simmental) is as extreme as comparing a Shetland Pony with a heavy horse like a Shire. Minnie could quite comfortably stand under Folly's belly, and there is a weight ratio of 1 to 4.

And so it is no wonder everyone feels safer with the Minnies and assumes they must be the easiest to manage. This is why so many people come to the farm believing that they would love to own a Dexter and visualise her almost as a pet on their little paddock. And let's face it, that was exactly my reason for buying Moorhen, (my original and first house cow). My dream did come true but not without its doubts, struggles and frustrations. If prospective purchasers try to assure me they will cope because they've kept goats and a Minnie will just be a step up, my heart sinks. I then have to spend hours trying to dissuade them, because they are concentrating on the dinky looks and not on what makes a Dexter tick.

Anyone who has kept both large and small dogs possibly understands what I'm getting at. Strange as it may seem, size is not a guarantee of ease of management. Small is not necessarily and automatically beautiful. Dexters rather like tough little terriers, are doughty characters and need very firm handling. They were originally mountain cattle used to a hard and independent life, requiring much intelligence and resourcefulness. And this still forms a large part of their make-up. Their strength of mind and will is also backed up by a physical might far beyond their size. It must be to do with being short and foursquare and having a low centre of balance. (In contrast, I was reading recently how easy it would have been to trip up and pull down a towering Tyrannosaurus Rex!)

I can recall many times when Mike and I have had titanic battles as we've attempted to administer some medicine or treatment to one or other of the Dexters. They have actually jumped up and down on all fours to fight us off and if we were trying to give them a drench, the word took on a new meaning – as we became soaked in wormer or our wellies filled up with liquid paraffin. (It made walking a novel experience, I can tell you!)

The miniature bulls can be really tough guys, keeping even the larger members of their harem in control, and beating up everything they meet. One such was Percy, who regularly picked a fight with the huge electricity pole which he passed night and morning on his way in and out of the fields. I don't know how it had upset him, but it has never been the same again and leans at a funny angle. He also used to tip over and push around a huge 20 cow place feeder, which holds ½ ton round straw bales, (and roared at the top of his voice as he did so!)

In contrast to this St Trinian-type behaviour, is the lumbering stolidness of Folly and Honey. They are gentle giants – Mrs Plods, who will let a little child lead them. Folly came to me as a two-week-old gawky calf, and immediately decided that I was not only Mum, but her best friend too. She followed me about, guzzling 4 litres of milk several times a day, and just wanted to be cuddled. I can't ever remember teaching her to lead, she just accepted the halter as a matter of course and came more readily, when called, than any dog. She is so quiet she can be artificially inseminated or checked by the vet, as she stands on the field. And that too, is how I've often milked her, because her udder holds 4 gallons – far too much for one calf, even though her babies are always huge. One such was Kelvin who weighed in at 135lbs at birth! She is reliable enough to be led anywhere, even amongst traffic (mind you, most cars would come off worse if they hit her!) One day when she and some youngsters got out onto the Lane, I first rounded the others up and then only had to call Folly for her to return (and this, despite the fact that she had to leave a delicious patch of grazing on the verge!) Now, no self-respecting Dexter would have come back like that – I'd probably still be trying to catch them.

I really have a lot to thank my 'Minnies' for, because by starting with Dexters, and especially Moorhen, and coping with them successfully, I feel I could face anything! They taught me so much about cow psychology, and how to manage bovine tantrums and bovine prima donnas. Those battles of mind (mine) over matter (bovine) were the best grounding I could ever have had.

As a result, coping with Honey was a doddle – she arrived on the scene as a 3-day-old calf bought in to double-suckle Folly and help me relieve that Great Udder! She was a delightful baby – very playful and full of fun. Now that she is a huge white Charolais cow, her cheerful nature is matched by a gentle sensitivity which makes you forget her great size, and certainly belies the idea that cows are dumb and unfeeling (I can assure you none are, and I hope Tippex's story will help to convince you). Honey's empathy with me is best illustrated by what happened when Mike became very ill. I used to spend a great deal of time working or just walking on the fields and I would go and pour my heart out to the cows. I often sat down with Honey, and leaning into the curve of her neck, I'd sob through all my troubles. She would then do an amazing thing – she would bring her head round and hold me tightly to her. (I actually can't think of a better place to die myself, than that).

You can see by this, that I know what's in Honey's heart and when I see her, it's not her bulk that I focus on at all. Such X-Ray vision is featured in 1 Samuel Chapter 16, where Samuel learns to see people as God sees us. Samuel had been sent to Jesse's house to anoint a King in place of Saul. He hadn't been told which son of Jesse (and he had 8) it was to be, so naturally Eliab the eldest was brought before him first. He was tall and handsome and Samuel thought, "Ah! Here's the one." But God said "No! you're looking at the outward appearance, but I'm looking at what's in a man's heart."

The next six boys in line were fetched in as possibilities, but God rejected them all, because He had chosen the 8th and youngest son, David, who Jesse had totally discounted and left looking after the sheep. Why was he the choice? Because his heart was right with God – and "he was a man after God's heart."

KLING-ON AND THE PUSSIES

'One man's garbage is another man's treasure' would have been the perfect motto for Mike if only I'd thought of it while he was alive. He could never throw anything away – much to my exasperation, and even rifled among other people's rubbish! He could find a use for the most unlikely scrap and Station Farm is held together by such waste materials! He went in for re-cycling in such a big way, that it became an art form. I am quite surprised that he never erected a notice at the farm entrance reading something like this: "Tip all you like here, please: **BY ORDER**". Mind you, he wouldn't really have needed to do so, because isolated country spots seem to be regarded by many as just the place for a rubbish dump.

I could give you a long and tedious itemised list of what we've found left on our 'doorstep', but I'll stick to some of the animate ones as examples.... 24 banties 'dropped' in our wood, 3 very ugly and aggressive cockerels left at the cow buildings, 2 large blousy hens put out on the lane, while the following were abandoned in and around the farm and garden; a dog, a small pretty and delightfully friendly cat, several ringed pigeons, tiny kittens, a terrified and heavily pregnant black cat and 150 store lambs (i.e. sheep-sized) which a villager kindly drove the mile to us, believing they were ours. I'm still waiting (and actually longing) for somebody to leave me an elephant – an animal I would dearly like to get to know. I'm sure someone out there is dying to get rid of one.

Usually I've given all the waifs and strays homes, there's room enough to be sure, but last winter I did begin to wonder if we were turning into a Cat Sanctuary. I hold Steel (my German Shepherd Dog) partly responsible, but someone somewhere must also take the blame. Steel's role was that of sniffer dog since with a nose as long as his, no smell is safe. He has unearthed untold creatures – families of hedgehogs, mice, voles, rabbits, stoats and rats (not a popular find with me) sitting pheasants and partridges (galore) and many bat colonies. He never harms them but just stands and barks in a silly falsetto voice to get my attention or dashes about peering in gaps and then rushes to fetch me. Last February he was engaged in one of these 'games' in the sheep house where many rats or bunnies hide under the portable feeder. They sit there in complete safety, teasing him, while his hysteria mounts. Usually after a day or two the 'quarry' moves house or Steel gives up, but on this occasion, each successive day he seemed more and more excited and to be trying harder than usual to tell me all about it.

In order to see beneath the feeder I have to get right down on my hands and knees and I don't usually bother, but this time I gave in. Rather gingerly in case 'ratty', being cornered, might bite, I took a peep. A little foot shot out defensively as Steel's nose joined mine. Whatever was it? Definitely not a rat or rabbit and anyway neither would use their foot in such a way. I'd got to get nearer. And there was a tiny, pathetic scrap of pussyhood, huddled in the hollow! Gathering it up, I rushed across to the house to have a proper look.

In the light I could see the kitten was so thin that every bone showed up, perhaps it had been under the feeder for days and oats and hay wouldn't have been much use to it. Its tummy, like those of starving pot-bellied children had become so distended that it dragged on the ground. Its eyes and nose were full of discharge, and its breathing was so laboured that it had to have cat flu and/or pneumonia at the very least. Despite all this, it was keen to eat (little and often) and full of character – unafraid and very happy to be snuggled up by the Rayburn. A double course of anti-biotics was to see it through its crisis and T.L.C. put the finishing touch to its recovery.

This kitten joined two other feline refugees who were by that time about seven-months old and considerably larger. Steel had found these and their brothers as three-week old waifs, abandoned on the farm when their feral mother was shot on neighbouring land. She had been dumped on us a year before, but was very timid and had dared not come to me. She had successfully reared a litter of kittens earlier in the year, refusing all help of food. She had already got these other mites on to some solid food and had trained them to be clean, as I was to discover. But if Big Nose had not sniffed them out, I would never have realised they were in the building, let alone in trouble. By the time rescue came, all were starving, one had hypothermia and needed reviving in the Rayburn Oven, two still needed feeding milk from a dropper and all were so young they could barely walk. For a week I took them up to my bedroom and fed them twice through the night, using warm milk kept in a thermos. And the first night was one I'll never forget.

After feeding all four, I put them back snug on their woolly jumper in a warm box and went back to bed. As I settled down, I realised there was a throbbing noise, like a car on the lane. Oh no! I thought, Thieves again! But why wasn't Steel barking? As I strained to hear better I realised it was no vehicle – it was **PURRING**! All four little mites, with full tummies, warmth and safety were cuddled together in bliss! That was a reward I'll treasure forever!

By the time Kling-on appeared on the scene I had found two of these kittens a lovely home together. The remaining brothers had settled in well here, become very tame and had grown into fine-looking cats. However, their feral origins have given them nervous temperaments, so for some time they regarded 'baby' in horror, as though he was an alien from another planet. This daft attitude, and the fact that he clung on desperately to my clothing when I held him, prompted me to name him **KLING-ON**. And as far as I was concerned he could have come from Outer Space! Actually I don't believe in U.F.O.'s.

Little-un was defensive to the point of aggression at first, desperately feeling he needed to fight for his food, his bed and my love. He used to throw his paws round his food dish, should the other cats approach, and bravely poke what to him was a giant of a dog on the nose, if he felt harassed. He had obviously lived in a tough home where he was kicked or knocked about because he was very nervous of my feet. I know they're big but although I only gently brushed against him one day, he cowered in a corner for ages afterwards and refused to be comforted.

It's several months since his arrival and Kling-on is transformed - fat, sleek, gentle and so laid-back you could think him lazy. All the aggression has gone and Steel now has his nose rubbed, not dabbed with a claw. It's lovely to see cat and dog in such harmony and greeting one another. And it is certain the kittens owe their lives to Steel, who they tend to hero-worship, since they see safety in his bulk and his courage. Cats have long memories so perhaps they know he has rescued them. They love to be with him, but unlike me, he is a bit embarrassed by the substitute Mother role. Kling-on in particular adores and trusts him. He has responded to T.L.C. in a big way. If he could write I'm sure he might well echo David's psalm of Deliverance which we find in No.27. David suffered so much rejection and fear at the hands of his enemies and family that he wrote "though my father and mother forsake me (and Kling-on's human substitute 'parents' certainly had too) the Lord will receive, literally <u>'gather up',</u> me." I really like this idea of being gathered up in God's arms, just as I did Kling-on, and then bore him to safety.

I'm sure Kling-on could echo David's assurance in God's care - verses 1-3, "whatever happens – even though war break out against me... I will be confident in the Lord's care". Of course for Kling-on, it is 'in Jenny's care', as I act as a steward for my Lord's creation.

DON'T LET GO

Most people who ride, choose horses as their mounts but who wants to be conventional? Sheep are for me – they're nearer to the ground, so there's less of a struggle climbing aboard. This is especially so if they dive helpfully between your legs and pick you up en route. Of course,  since they are usually on their way to the food trough or a rendezvous with the ram you may have no choice of destination. But you mustn't complain because it is always an exciting mystery tour, pursued at high speed with a spectacular finish. Landing head first amidst the rugby scrum of woolly bodies all trying to get at their tea, is an invigorating experience and not to be missed if you have a taste for adventure.

I have always been a glutton for this sort of thing. In my teens riding was my passion and I was sure I had a 'way' with horses. I had – but not quite as I fondly imagined. Any horse meeting me, took one look and thought, "Ah! Here's a sucker! She'll let me do ANYTHING". As a result I was terribly good, not at actually riding, but at falling off! In fact, I became an expert at it. I could fall off at high speed, at the trot or even when we were stationary. My instructor had long since given me up as a hopeless case. She had but one piece of advice, it was: "Don't let go of those reins." This was yelled through gritted teeth often with a few other well-chosen words added! So I was dragged through brambles, hedges, puddles, haystacks **BUT**, I am proud to say, I <u>NEVER</u> LET GO. However, I have to admit my instructor was not the slightest bit impressed. I rather wish she could see my efforts now – she might change her mind. Thanks to her good schooling, I'm awfully adept at leading cows about on halters because nothing (well, almost nothing!) will loosen my grip of their ropes. So, those early horsey experiences stood me in very good stead once I became a cowperson. Having purchased a completely unhandleable 'House Cow' straight off the `open plains' as it were, certain matters needed sorting out, mostly in <u>her</u> mind, not mine.

First of all despite her title, a House Cow does <u>not</u> enter your house (if you can help it). Mine did try to get in via our open bedroom window one never-to-be-forgotten morning. We lived in a bungalow at that point and often over-slept and she had decided that it was high time for her breakfast. She was also lonely as she had been wrenched away from her relatives and friends to live alone in our garden with just us for company. It was a severe culture shock and she coped with it by adopting me as her surrogate herd and family. This meant that when she spotted me, either lying in bed, or in the garden she mooed "Hello". She also bellowed "Goodbye" as I left her and then yelled "Where are you?" over and over again when I'd disappeared. We and our neighbours had a very noisy time, but her attachment to me was a huge asset to sorting out a second vital matter.

At 6-years old she had to learn halter training and I had wondered however I was going to get her to accept leading, essential if I was to take her up the lane to a friend's little field, let alone tie her up for milking. I need never have worried; she was only too eager to follow me - <u>anywhere</u>. In a week, she'd learnt her name (I'd quickly better tell you that she was called Woodmagic Moorhen because as a pedigree Dexter she'd been in a herd called after birds! – friends later corrupted this to Moo-hen). She also learnt commands like **WAIT,** (as traffic passed) and helpfully stretched out her head for the halter (and of course, a tit-bit). I only wish I could train a dog as easily!

As time went on, familiarity bred contempt in Moorhen, and she was quite liable to try turning off the lane, to dive through a hedge into some luscious sugar beet, or someone's hay field and dance around angrily because she hadn't managed to shake me off. When we returned from our outings I often looked as though I'd been through a hedge backwards, because I actually <u>had</u>, but **I NEVER LET GO!**

Once our herd grew and we had moved to my present farm I was well used to training cattle to lead and it was a saleable asset. All heifers were led about from babyhood so, for example, I thought nothing of leading two well-grown heifers together one in each hand. One evening I decided to take Emma and Amber, who were very biddable, across the lane from one part of the farm to the other. All went well, till we reached the sloping track which leads to the cow yards. Here the neighbours' Bull Mastiff dog was prowling about. At the sight of him, both heifers stiffened. I tightened my grip on their ropes and gently tried to encourage them forward. I also called out to Bodger to "sit". He completely ignored me and came straight for us all. It was no good, Amber and Emma had had enough. Both decided to set off, as fast as possible, but in opposite directions. I tried hard to hang on, as they gathered speed, but my arms couldn't take the strain. The 6cwt pull on each rope broke my golden rule as I fell flat on my face. Anyway the heifers knew the way to their loose boxes and I caught them up eventually.

On other occasions, like T.B. testing days or when cows used to be artificially inseminated there have been titanic struggles to keep a grip on their halters. I have usually managed to hold on, despite being trampled in quagmires, squashed against walls or tipped into water tanks. My 'heroic' efforts have given so-called 'friends' much amusement but I shall always cherish the remark made by two little boys as they admired one of my more successful attempts: "Cor! Look at her. Isn't she brave! She's still got hold of that bull!" (It was actually an in-milk cow with a very full udder, but they were near the front end.)

I do have to own up to one utter failure in the "hold fast" stakes and this occasion had nothing whatever to do with animals. We were having a week's holiday on the Broads, on a hired half-decker. After sailing all one morning, we decided to moor for lunch at Ranworth. As we came in, the crew (me) had orders to fend off other boats and jump up onto the jetty. Unfortunately, a fickle breeze made us unexpectedly lurch onto a near-by yacht, neatly squashing my thumb between the two boats. Once on land, as I prepared to tie us up to a bollard, I inadvertently glanced at my hand. The sight made me yelp dramatically and drop the rope.

As Michael floated helplessly away, his protests were drowned by the chatter from a crowd who'd gathered round me to get a glimpse of the gory wound. Yes! I <u>know</u>! I'd broken **THE RULE,** but after 12 stitches and some weeks of throbbing agony, I felt a bit justified. Still, even after all these years I can feel guilty at letting both Mike and the rope down.

Whatever relevance has all this to our Christian lives? Well, in the book of Revelation John wrote these words from our Lord Jesus to both the Church at Thyatira and Philadelphia Rev. 2.25 and 3.11. "Hold fast (i.e. don't let go) to what you have till I come... so no one takes your crown". Here's a clear golden rule. God's grace and blessings are far too precious to hold on to lightly, and far, far too precious to forfeit! He urges us to have disciplined souls which will hold fast and press on to His goal for us, as Paul says in Philippians 3.14, "never letting go of our grip on the eternal crown which is ours." Such a prize in Glory is surely worth all the rope burns, scratches, squashed thumbs, indignities and wounds that we will suffer in His name. Christians **DON'T LET GO.**

SUSIE

Susie has such stunning looks that Stanley (the Bull) is 'putty in her hands', even if one of her hooves is rather twisted.

However, the cows who have impeccable pedigrees treat her with scorn (and probably a good bit of envy). "Well my dear!" they must say, "who does she think she is? What ghastly family connections!"

Her Grandma is in fact an aristocratic dun-coloured Dexter, called Coral, but her Grandad, despite going by the impressive name of Weston Jamaica was one of those Murray Greys! A made-up breed if ever there was one! To make matters worse her parents were both Murray Grey Xs (crosses), so she is therefore a Murray Grey XX!

She has somehow triumphed over all these breeding gaffes, and become one of the most eye-catching members of the herd. She has inherited her neat, foursquare build from Coral, but her crowning glory has come from her Grandpa's line. This is her silky, pale silver grey coat, the best shade that the Murrays fall heir to. Many of the others turn out to be darker, with tightly frizzed wiry fur so that they look rather like walking Brillo Pads. (You can imagine what the cows think of them!)

Susie has also received the naturally polled (hornless) Murray head, delicately sculptured in her case and fringed with a mass of lustrous waves. And of course she has to have the longest bovine eye lashes I've ever see, which flutter across large, limpid eyes. When she blossomed into such a gorgeous teenager, Stanley soon made sure she was in the family way. But I hardly dare tell you that her baby will be a Murray Grey XXX – too dreadful for the cows to contemplate – a shudder will go through the whole herd at its birth.

As if all these physical attributes were not enough, Susie is actually a very nice animal! She made herself tame when quite young, by following me about and asking for a fuss, and so she quickly learnt her name. She's always got time for people, even complete strangers, whereas many of the cattle ignore visitors and rudely stomp off. I expect they think – "Oh there's Teacher's Pet again! Sucking up to someone else now!" I have a sneaking feeling that they might almost have been glad the day that disaster struck her. It happened when I took some friends out to meet the herd and Susie led the rush to greet us.

Once everyone began to peel off and graze, I noticed Susie was lying down and making no attempt to follow. She was in distress, but I couldn't make out what was wrong. I soon did, on my return to the field sometime later; she was on her feet, but could barely move. To my horror I found that she had broken a front leg, just above her hoof – probably caught it in a rabbit hole during the stampede earlier. This was a terrible discovery, and spelt Doom for her – the usual treatment is humane slaughter either on farm or at the butchers. But such an outlook was unthinkable – I loved her, Stanley loved her, she was a Mum-to-be and I'd got to save her.

You're perhaps thinking that a death sentence is too drastic for a broken bone, surely they soon heal? Yes, if you can immobilise the limb and splint it. But that is almost impossible for cattle, and the stress of the fixed leg would be worse than the pain of leaving it alone. And being a front foot is worse because it has to be load-bearing as the animal rises. She has to lean all her weight on her knees while standing up on her hind legs. How could Susie cope with the agony of getting up and down? I decided to get some <u>very</u> strong pain killers from the vet and see if these would help her get about to feed.

Once I had them I had to devise a way of giving them to her without the others coming over for a share and beating her up. As she was hungry, I decided to cut her some lawn-mowings and tip the powders on to the grass, and persuade her to take them like this. I could not let the herd see me bearing a bucket of food – a suicidal action. So, I put on an old anorak of Mike's which has very large pouch pockets, stuffed them full of mowings and went in to Susie while she was lying down. Putting a handful of grass in front of her nose, I quickly tipped a powder on the heap, and hoped I'd not been spotted by the rest of the cattle. I managed this for 4 days and Susie's pain was obviously much less and she could graze for short periods.

For two or three weeks, she hobbled slowly about swinging her poor leg uselessly along, but after a month she began putting her weight on it. Now, three months on, she is running and even keeping up with the bunch. There is a large mass of bone around the break, which has spoilt her once slim ankle, but she barely limps at all.

Though that Black Monday had spelt evil for Susie and had seemed an unmitigated disaster, much good came out of it. First, it brought us closer, she loved the extra attention and became even more handleable. Next, it seemed to make her even more placid and biddable. And last, but by no means least, it sealed her future with me. (I had rather reluctantly planned to sell her once she calved because I am over-stocked and must not keep any young heifers). Now, of course, I cannot part with her in such a crippled state and so instead of an uncertain prospect (you can never guarantee finding a good home) she is here till her dying day.

Her experience illustrates Joseph's words to his brothers in Genesis 50.20 "You intended to harm me but God intended it for good..." And of course there's the same thought in Romans 8.28 "We know that in all things God works for the good of those who love Him..." And as Christians we don't need to have to be very old to look back on life and see that what seemed like total disasters worked out to far greater blessings as God's hand directed events.

Susie so loved and trusted me that she humbly accepted what had happened to her, convinced I knew best and would do what was best. Now our all-wise, all-loving Father <u>does</u> know best. He'll lead us on through everything – His eternal plans for us are too deep and wonderful to be understood now. He asks us to trust Him even though we cannot see the outcome any more than Susie could, and even though we don't like what is happening. "Even though we walk through the valley of the shadow of death", we are walking ever homewards to "be always with Christ which is far better".Phil. 1.23.

We do not know what lies ahead,
But we know who holds the future,
With God things don't just happen,
Everything by him is planned.
So as I face tomorrow
With its problems large and small,
I'll trust the God of miracles,
Give to Him my all.

No. 269 Mission Praise.

HOME, SWEET HOME

"Oh! To have the gift to see ourselves as others see us", may have been okay for Robbie Burns to wish, but he was obviously not a stockman/woman or he'd never have said that. You see, I know that my cows, sheep, bantams, dogs and cats have a far from flattering view of me. Basically, I'm a walking food trolley –

parsnip or carrot shaped, clothed in hay, with hair of straw, as far as the cattle and ewes are concerned. I look like a sack of wheat in the banties' eyes, while the dogs and cats see me as tin-shaped. And all of them picture me within a frame which is house-shaped, because I offer them safety and shelter. As a result, unlike many farmers who find it difficult to keep their stock at home, I just can't seem to shake mine off!

This became evident years ago when we tried our hand at goat-keeping. Our nanny was so attached to me, that nothing would keep her from my side. Tethers and fences were broken so that she could wait outside our door, ready to seize her chance of joining me indoors. On going outside, I would find her pushing past me as she dashed into the hall. This was rather narrow and long and she could not be persuaded to turn round and go out the way she'd come. There was nothing for it but to lead her all the way through the bungalow and out the back door. Such devotion was touching I know, but somewhat inconvenient. Especially as she was far from house-trained and being indoors made her nervous!

Sheep, like goats, are great home lovers and I nearly hung up one of those stitched and framed "Home Sweet Home" pictures in their sheep house. Their beloved building is their bolt-hole and utterly essential to their peace of mind. Mine use their house all year round – for shelter and lambing at night, in winter and spring and for daytime shade in the summer.

Sheep also have a very powerful 'hefting' (homing) instinct; this is especially so if they are close to their shepherd or if they belong to certain breeds like Herdwicks for example. These sheep also teach their daughters all their grazing haunts and even if they are sold away will return by hook or by <u>crook</u>.

Recently I heard of three sheep sold from Yorkshire to Kent who walked all the way back home!!

I can't claim such a feat for any of mine, but one sunny autumn afternoon they showed how they love their home. They were over ½ mile away strip-grazing a neighbour's stubble field and had plenty of food; so with no worries about them I was sitting in the sun with my feet up for a while. I'd nearly dozed off, when a lot of scuffling at my gate alerted me. And there were the 50 strong flock, gathered in the lane, all demanding to be let into the garden. They'd broken down their temporary fence, after being panicked by something, and with one mind had come home, to find me.

Cattle too love their home and its security and if you keep a single cow, as we did at first, they become as close to you as any faithful dog. Moorhen, my house cow who we kept before we began farming, was a constant companion of mine. I'd taught her to lead about on the verges and friends' large gardens when we were short of grazing. I just tagged along on the end of the rope watching her enjoy all sorts of goodies from nuts, fallen pears and apples to weeds. She hoovered and pruned while I talked to her, fussed over her and day-dreamed. We spent hours in each others company. The strength of the bond between us was high-lighted one memorable lunch time. At the time, we had our bungalow up for sale, as we were planning to move to our present farm. Prospective buyers were supposed to view by appointment, but, of course, people often turned up unannounced, even though we were tucked well away.

A couple had suddenly decided to appear in this way and I spotted them drive up while I was with Moorhen a quarter of a mile distant on a friend's lawn. I decided I'd better run back to see them and telling Moorhen to 'wait' I dashed off. I reached the visitors as they were gingerly stepping through our garden-cum-paddock. Their smart summer foot-wear was not really up to such a trek, and showed an unfamiliarity with rural ways. Their first question revealed yet more ignorance of life in remote Norfolk backwaters. "Were we on mains gas?" they enquired.

Mains Gas! We'd only had mains water and electricity a few years before (neither of which were even on at the farm we were buying!) Mains Gas would never reach such outlying areas – the cost of the pipelines was too prohibitive. Our Electricity even came in by over-head lines and was inclined to give up the ghost at the first hint of a gale or blizzard. As I began trying to explain all this the sound of thundering hooves reached us. The noise got nearer and nearer until Moorhen suddenly appeared round the corner of the gateway, hurtling towards us! I caught her rope and pulled her up, and then turned to reassure the couple. But they were fleeing to their car and once in, they drove off without a backward glance.

Moorhen, in terror, had realised she was **ALL ALONE** and needing me, she'd come back to the safety of home. But the couple must have seen the event in a very different light – they'd probably feared at least a goring by an enraged bull that this mad woman seemed to be keeping in her garden, and not surprisingly they never appeared again.

Having wryly reminisced about my animals' rather touching attachment to their home, I've remembered the quote from Robbie Burns again. What about my human friends' view of me? Well, I'd rather not go into details (!) but I will reveal one thing. I'm just as firmly bound to my home as any of the sheep. I've never been on holiday for 25 years and the only nights I've spent away from the farm in that time were three, when I was in hospital. I'm not telling you this to excite your pity, because I can honestly say I don't want to go anyway and I could never think of leaving the care of the stock to anyone else for longer than a day. I am very privileged to live in a beautiful spot with acres to roam and a wild coast close-by where I can sail for an hour or so on the tide (if I've the time). My friends see me as a complete vegetable who's stuck-in-the-mud, but rural Norfolk has this contenting effect on me (and many others). I know of some folk who have quite happily hardly ever left the village of their birth, nor strayed far. On the days I have to travel I always yearn to return home, as quickly as possible. Much as I love my home here, I know that "there is a place/home being prepared for me" in heaven which will be far, far better. Why can I be sure? Because Jesus said so, while he was with His disciples. And He even added this to reassure us: "If it were not so, I would have told you". John 14. He knew we would have doubts and added this to help us. Time and time again this has bolstered my wavering faith in Him. It has such a ring of truth. So as Christians we can be sure and certain that "we will dwell in the House of the Lord for ever" Psalm 23.6 – i.e. we shall be "forever with the Lord" and in his presence. And the word "house" here in the original text has a homely meaning, as does the word "place prepared" – we shall be 'at home' with our Father – comfortable and able to be ourselves, rather like wearing a loved old pair of slippers. The 'pull' of God's home, rivals even the hold that the farm has on me. So I can say with David, "My soul yearns, even faints for the courts of the Lord". Psalm 84.2

ANGELS IN DISGUISE

Us Sparks are supposed to be noted for flying upwards (Job 5.7) but in my case, I let the side down. It is because, both the 'flying' and 'upwards' bits, set my knees quaking and my head spinning. I have never understood the desperate urge which drove poor Icarus on to fly. Why ever did he <u>want</u> to take wings and take such risks? My feet of clay are quite happy to be stuck in Station Farm's mud and never leave the ground. Then I think of those intrepid characters (Jessica at 19 being one of them!) who actually throw themselves off a cliff or mountain top relying on just a flimsy layer of material to hang glide or parascend. Don't they know that what goes up must come down? And it's the coming down that can be so tricky and the ground so hard.

I have to admit that I can't even <u>walk</u> down a mountain side without problems. In fact, I'm probably the only person who has descended Mt. Nissen (in Switzerland) on my behind. It was fine going upwards on this occasion, since the climb to 8,000ft, was stiff but gentle. However, I forgot that I would have to face the other way as I went down! I couldn't take the view and promptly sat down and only got to my feet once I was safely in the valley again.

Faced with running the farm on my own, there was one daily task which filled me with dread. It was the fetching down of bales of straw and hay from the stacks. The latter can be up to 25ft high and the wise move is to keep 'steps' in the face of them, so that you can get up and down fairly safely. Even this method gives me the jitters. If something goes wrong and you need to use the ladder to reach the top bale it really can be quite dangerous. I've always tried to get round this problem by pulling bales down with a rake or pole, but of course, a falling bale is heavy enough to badly injure or even kill someone. So it is a silly thing to do and especially if the bantams have made a nest on top which you don't know about. That kind of egg shampoo is not to be recommended!

One afternoon during my first winter alone, I was forced to use the ladder arrangement and also had to put it at a very steep angle.

Although I climbed up successfully, it was a different story when I put my foot on the rung to go down. The ladder slid away and I just managed to scramble back! I now couldn't reach the ladder and the sides of the stack were sheer and the whole lot was rather wobbly. Down below me, Shiva looked up and wagged her tail – if only she could get help! But who was around to help? I have only one permanent neighbour and even if he were home he would never hear for he was at least ¼ mile away. I wondered if I dared to try scrambling down, but the thought of the concrete floor quickly put that idea out of my head. Then I began to freak out and had to get right back against the barn wall and sit down. I was stuck. It was nearly the cows' tea-time and I didn't know what to do. Oh for a mobile phone! But wait, I thought, I do have one, with the largest possible range and hooked up to the best Emergency Service in the world. So I sent up a 999 call to Our Father God. Without His intervention I might have been there yet. What happened next was a very unusual 'coincidence' – I've used that word, because that's how many would see it. However, I prefer to call it a God-incidence and a very quick response to my S.O.S.

As I huddled up on the bales in a complete tizzy I heard the noise of a tractor approaching. Nothing strange in that of course, the neighbouring farmer frequently sends his tackle along the lane. But this one was slowing down... Should I yell out? No! the driver would never hear me where I was, deep in the barn and well away from the road. Then I made out sounds of manoeuvring and finally the engine was switched off.

Whoever was it? Why had they stopped? A few minutes later I could make out someone calling my name and Shiva set off to see who was there and to bark a warning. She quickly returned bringing the visitor with her. As he called out again, I recognised David's voice – a good friend who farms in a near-by village and does work like hay-making for me too. Still not daring to stand up, or look down, I told him where I was and what had happened. As he doesn't like heights either, he could sympathise with me and had soon propped up the ladder and seen me down safely. We then laughed it all off because he has a lovely sense of humour which quickly defuses a tense situation. But I'm sure he didn't realise what an 'angel' in disguise he'd been. Why had he come just at that moment? Well, he was driving home along the top lane (another ¼ - ½ mile off) when the machinery he was pulling, broke. He could not take it the 3 miles home, so he had decided to drag it down to me and leave it on my track. Such an event has never happened before or since in nearly 20 years, and it was a wonderful answer to my 999 call. God's emergency service is certainly speedy as I had found out.

Another event which took place a couple of years afterwards was to reinforce this discovery. This time it was to involve Andrew, David's son who with his father runs their arable and cattle enterprise. It was a hot summer's afternoon, so the cows were particularly thirsty and I had to set off to fill their water tanks yet again. They were on the 25 acre field about a half mile away from the farm. As I walked down to them I could see Percy the Bull and April were courting. Several herd members were also tagging along like gooseberries, and there was much jumping and dancing about. Once I was in with them I turned to pull the water pipe from the hedge bottom and out from under the electric fence. Here I met a **BIG SNAG**. The three lines of wire were on the ground, along with a fence post which should have been holding them up! It had been snapped like a matchstick (probably by the antics of the courting couple). It is a sad fact that the inanimate objects on the farm are as good at falling down as I am, much preferring to be grounded – <u>eight</u> trees once fell down during a winter hurricane for example. This post had also chosen a very bad time to let me down and why ever the cattle had not escaped already I did not know. They soon would, if I didn't <u>do</u> something, for a group of youngsters were breathing down my neck as they eagerly eyed the gap.

Once I had pulled the fence upright again, I stopped to think. This was all very well as long as I held on, but what would happen if I let go and went off for some tools? I didn't even have a scrap of bailer twine in my pockets. If I'd had some, I might have been able to temporarily secure the post to the hedge. If only Steel could fetch things for me instead of just sitting and watching. And I still didn't own a mobile phone! What I needed was a Heavenly sky hook, and I had to call on God's 999 service yet again. Almost at once Steel barked! Someone was about! And there was Andrew peering through the hedge saying "Hallo". He had been on my other field pulling weed beet out of the crop growing there. He'd been doing so for most of the day, unknown to me and was about to go home for tea when he had spotted me. Don't think by the way that such a task is a daily occurrence, so that Andrew would be on the field frequently. No, on the contrary, this was the <u>only</u> day in the summer he would do so since it is a one-off thing. And a few minutes later he'd have left for home. This was a perfectly timed God-incidence, and I could hand over the post to the 'angel' in disguise while I scuttled off for a repair outfit.

I'm sure all of us can think of similar happenings to these, but it's very easy to dismiss them and not give God the praise and glory. David's life as recorded in 1 and 2 Samuel is full of such rescues as God saved him from so many dire situations. And his Psalms reflect God's care in his troubled times and how he had found that "God was his refuge and strength an ever-present help in trouble" Ps.46.1. And in Ps. 34.7, he wrote "The angel of the Lord encamps around those who fear Him and He delivers them".

We will most probably never see an angel in glowing splendour, but many "have entertained angels unawares" Hebrews 13.2. For as a fine old hymn states:- "His angels here are human, not the shining hosts above".

("There's a light upon the mountain", No. 679 Mission Praise). And His angels here are just as much part of His plans; so in a crisis we now know what to do (in trusting faith, of course). "Call upon Me in the day of trouble, I will deliver you and you will honour Me". Psalm 50.15.

DESIGNER TRAINING

Mounted on the gable end of the sheep house is a very special weather vane. It is a steam train, pointing out the wind's direction by its smoke and its erection was one of the last projects Mike undertook before he finally went into hospital. He chose it because not only was he mad about steam engines, but also because it was an emblem for Station Farm. (The old Station by the way, is now a home and a mile long railway embankment is one of my boundaries.) The station was also a mile from the village, with no houses in between. So anyone wanting to use the train before Beeching struck, had to be in-<u>training</u> to walk here. Young and old, fit or fat had to be able to do the distance.

Today, walking that far is almost unthinkable – out comes the car instead. But in actual fact, for those who are caught up in the fitness craze, it would have been an ideal and useful jog, as part of the journey to work and back. A sort of 'training' scheme in all senses. Anyone in earnest to run say a marathon must have a carefully planned and structured routine which builds up to the event. Indeed it is true for any similar activity from a tennis championship to horse racing – however for the latter the animal's training must be parallel to the human's and just as thorough. Here on the farm, the cows have long been at pains to lick their cowsbody into good shape, so that their teas will be served at the double. (While I have been deluded into thinking I am training them!)

Do people really try to train cows, some of you must be asking in disbelief! If you are imagining that I am aiming for the kind of athletic prowess needed for the nursery rhyme that claims: "the cow's jumped over the moon"... even I know that's going to be difficult. In fact, I could re-write the words more on these lines:

"Hey diddle, diddle, the cat's on the fiddle
(in my larder again!)
The cow's jumped out of the field".

And that's precisely why cattle can benefit from a bit of discipline. You may by now be feeling that I'm a bit of a spoil sport, but prevention is better than cure as I'll try to explain in a while. So how does one go about training a cow? Not, surprisingly, by turning the barn into a gym for their work-outs, although you'll see later that they have tried to change my mind over this. No; basically the way to a cow's heart (and obedience) is through her stomachs - but – there's much more to it than that. Ideally a relationship must be developed between you and her, as with Moorhen and I, based on love and trust (though of course, any animal can be controlled with harshness and force instead). Over the years I have 'trained' all my herd, heifers and bullocks as well as cows, which often number 30 and have been as high as 50. In its simplest form the education programme, started from the earliest baby days, includes talking to them, using their names, and making a fuss of them if they are amenable. So the cattle are people-friendly unlike most suckler herds which are left to their own devices and very wary of strangers. Jessica, a young friend who has been coming to the farm for several years, helps in this handling of the cattle and will even brush and groom any who appreciate this. If there is a need to train an individual to a halter and being led, perhaps say for showing or hand-milking, then he or she must be singled out and even separated from the herd. I can illustrate this by telling you Woodmagic Tui's story. This little Dexter heifer had become too much of a handful for her owner. She had come out of the same herd as Moorhen when only a calf and although she had been hand-reared, no kind of relationship had been built up at the same time. So she grew up in the company of an unruly and dimwitted Jersey bull calf and the pair of them developed a deep distrust of human beings. In a moment of madness I agreed to buy her, assured by the Artificial Insemination certificate that she was in-calf and could go straight in with my pregnant heifers.

Once I was home the doubts and questions I should have voiced before I wrote the cheque for her purchase came flooding into my mind. How on earth could her owner have caught her and kept her still and under control long enough to be inseminated? It also seemed amazing that her 'bulling' had even been noticed – you see, it is essential to catch a maiden heifer at the peak of her short (24 hour) heat. I would need to watch her closely and I would also need to get her handleable in case she needed the Artificial Insemination services again. So before she arrived the next day, I decided to prepare a place for her in a separate building. Then as I fed her, I'd be able to try haltering her at the same time.

Well, despite her great nervousness, within a couple of days, I'd managed to slip a rope on her as she ate and had even been able to stroke and brush her. By the next day I felt I could risk leading her out to a bucket of food which I placed by a tether in a rich piece of grazing. Now most cattle finding themselves chained and restricted in this way will throw themselves about for a while, so I stayed with her for most of that morning. In fact, she behaved very quietly and enjoyed her feed of grass. I repeated this method for some days, while her trust in me grew, and haltering and tying up became a habit for her.

I was very glad I had done so because by the following week as I was innocently bent down feeding her, she suddenly mounted me! Yes, she had come bulling as I'd guessed she might do. But, this time she would stand still and the service was likely to be successful...

Within a fortnight I felt Tui was well enough acquainted with Station Farm methods to meet the rest of my cattle and she was released to join them all. After that I could always catch her when needed and she was people-imprinted.

Such training gives cattle a head start for finding a good, caring home if they have to be sold on, due to overstocking for example. Even a cross-bred heifer has more of a chance of being bought for breeding by someone who will love her.

Obviously, animals within large suckler herds of over a hundred or more, have to be sold through sales and/or markets, and are rounded up en-masse and crushed for any handling. 'Crushed'? you're thinking – crushed concrete, crushed oats, but crushed cows?! Well, this means confining and firmly restraining them with a **VERY STRONG** metal frame with a head yoke etc. (if a 'Folly' enters one she is indeed a bit crushed, but a 'Minnie' rattles round like a pea in a pod, and would be better in a commercial calf crush!) Such temporary caging is essential for the safety of man and beast, because at three-quarters of a ton, a large cow or bull can bend thick metal bars as easily as Uri Geller can supposedly bend spoons.

But to get back to the Academy for Nice Young Cows here at Station Farm. What standards are they expected to achieve? They do not have to learn to read, although many visitors, seeing the names of Moorhen, Amber, Emma, and Beryl carved in wood above the old stalls those cows used to obediently enter for tea, have believed they do! They do not have to pass any exams and nor do I have to do any marking (thank goodness). But they do have to come when they're called and accept handling and instructions especially where I am trying to prevent a minor hitch turning into a major disaster. And this is where we come to the attempt the herd made to turn the barn into a sports centre, one winter's afternoon. During the months of November through to April, they are housed overnight in a large yard and a set of loose boxes. The latter are part of a huge traditional brick and tile building and there is a connecting door from them into the main area which is as big as a church. Here much of their hay and feed is stacked and so it is easy for me to take from there to their racks in the yard. Before I let them in at tea-time I check all is ready and lock the connecting door. Well, of course, it was inevitable that there would come a day when I'd forget to do so.

I was back across the lane seeing to some sheep near the house, when I realised my mistake. Loud and excited moos instead of the usual peace, while they munch through their tea, made me drop everything and run. When I reached the barn, I found a sort of mock bullfight was in progress. Bales from the stacks were being tossed and 'gored' amidst much gallumping about as others practised sprinting to and fro. Some of the cows, keen to show off their strength, had burst through the closed double doors which give access to the outside.

Putting on my best school-teacher voice, I yelled at them all, especially at individuals like Abba, Crystal and Coral who were already outside. Hearing their names they stopped in their tracks, and looked relieved to see me. They were beginning to dither and panic, knowing they'd got things wrong and were glad to turn round. They and the rest in the barn allowed themselves to be chivvied back into their yard, with no more problems. Their 'training' saved the day and probably saved me hours of frustrated chasing about.

Break-outs by suckler herds quite regularly occur and it can be very difficult, if not impossible to round everyone up. The animals get lost and terrified and I've known occasions when a plane has been hired to locate them and even shoot errant cattle who have been on the loose for weeks! To avoid that sort of situation, any training is worth all the effort involved. So for their best interests and to enable them to reach their full potential I try to mould my cows (like you would children) into an ideal which will fit them for life both here and in other homes.

If by God's grace we are His children, He will mould/conform us to the likeness of His son (Romans 8.29) and we can then say with Paul "by God's grace I am what I am" (1 Corinthians. 15.10). This could seem to imply that we need to make no effort, but in 1 Timothy 4.7 we find Paul saying "train yourself to be godly" (i.e. to become

Christ-like). The Greek word for train is **GUMNAZO**, and is the root of our word, gymnasium. This then suggests a very active and disciplined role for us and very much fits in with our present-day fitness craze.

In other words we should be going through a daily work-out for God, to keep our faith from going flabby. Co-operating daily with Him in regular spiritual exercise which would then underline His training scheme for each of us. And we're not just aiming for a rosette at some show like my cows, but an eternal prize, which is worth going through any pain threshold.

SHIVA

Shiva was the first German Shepherd Dog we ever owned and came to us as a delightful 12 week old puppy. She was gentle and biddable, quickly removing any fears I had about whether or not I'd cope with training and controlling her. German Shepherd Dogs, or Alsatians (two names for the same breed) are just like any other dog – with a leg at each corner, a nose at the front and a tail behind, and with exactly the same needs as a tiny Yorkie or a giant Irish Wolfhound. All need love, firmness and control. Even a Chihuahua can take you over, and I know of a couple who were into Spaniels (soppy endearing souls usually), whose house became ruled so totally by their latest Cocker, that he took control of their bedroom and refused to allow them to get to bed!

I need never have worried about managing Shiva for she was a timid individual who never left my side and preferred to keep out of trouble. She was perfectly safe with the livestock, sensibly avoiding the cows and being so terrified of the sheep, that, sheep worried her! Admittedly she had been beaten up by a ram as a puppy, but it was little lambs who sent her completely to pieces. When I had to bring half-dead babies indoors who needed warming up or urgent care, she became a duddering jelly and hid upstairs! Her nervousness meant she <u>had</u> to be near me if possible, so where I went she went. She always travelled with me and this included our weekly trips to the particular vegetable washing and packing works we were using at that time. Our trailing equipage (as Mike liked to call it) consisted of a very aged Land Rover, with a reluctance to start and an even greater one to actually keep going, and an aged home-made trailer based on a positively antique caravan chassis. When loaded we pulled home 2 tons, us and the dog, and on one never to be forgotten day an aged uncle too. This extra weight was too much for Land Rover and it conked out never to go again and we all had to be towed home by long-suffering friends with a powerful 4x4. 'All' meant 1½ tons of carrots, the trailer, the Land Rover, aged uncle, us and the dog!!

Before this ignominious event, we had gone as usual to the washer and Mike and I were engrossed in transferring roots from a waste trailer to our own. Shiva had come with us and been let out for a potter, while we were busy. After about ¼ of an hour, it dawned on me that I hadn't seen her for a long while. Calling and whistling, I looked about, but there was no dog bounding towards me.

Wherever was she? I got down from the trailer and went into the packing shed, as she did occasionally go to the men and women for a fuss. But no-one had seen her; nor had the chap in charge of the washing machinery outside. He then began to tell me how they were overrun with rabbits and several had been shot and fallen into the slurry pit. This is a large miry 'lake', where thousands of gallons of washing water, along with soil and rotten vegetables drain and collect. It's not a very pleasant spot as you can imagine and rotting carrots have a particularly unforgettable smell.

I thought I'd wander round it and work my way back to our trailer in that direction. Once I was away from the noise of the machinery I started calling Shiva again and it was then that I heard a weird sort of whine-cum-whimper – some kind of animal was in distress. One of the rabbits perhaps? I hurried towards the sound and found it was coming from the 'lagoon'. Then I saw a slight movement; something was struggling in the water. It was Shiva! – her head barely above the sludge as she feebly groped with one paw at the bank. But the pull of the mire was too much and she sank beneath the surface.

My heart raced – how was I going to get her out? The sides of the pit were sheer and she was a big dog – 80 – 90 lbs in weight – and her fur would be sodden. She would also be terrified and would struggle violently. (She had once nearly drowned me in the sea, when she got out of her depth and had clung to my back like a sinking man. I still have the scars of her claws on me.) How was I going to haul her out and not end up in the same position as she was in? I also had no idea how deep the pit was or how strong the pull of the mire. I cannot really remember it all clearly, except that I lay full length on the top of the bank and somehow reached her collar and neck chain. For a while I pulled and nothing happened; then I think Shiva made another effort to get out and between us she got both front legs up and the rest was easy. Grappling with her had encased me in sludge and she then made sure I was fully covered by shaking herself heartily! We both looked and smelt so appallingly bad that when Mike saw us he was speechless. He wasn't too keen on having to take us home (and was probably wondering if Land Rover would refuse to start on principle). As he drove, he had to keep putting his head out of the window for air.

We could think of only one way of effectively cleaning the pair of us and that was to use a hose. So, much to the amusement of a couple riding past on the lane, Michael hosed and scrubbed until Shiva's fur (instead of being grey) was black and gold again, and my features became recognisable once more. It was some days, despite baths for me and more washes for Shiva, before the terrible stench began to fade, and we were fit for society again.

Shiva's predicament was one of her own making; she had doubtless seen the tempting rabbit remains lying on the top of the slurry and thinking the surface was solid and to be trusted had run for them. The shock when, what she had assumed to be terra firma, had given way must have been dreadful. Especially as she (in common with most German Shepherd Dogs) did not like water. She had put her trust in 'sinking sand', as so many of us have done in our lives – 'sands' like wealth, a marriage or a 'secure' job, only to find these seemingly dependable foundations can collapse and fail us overnight. If we've been using these ephemeral bases for our life's support we will be as shocked as Shiva was. Only the Lord Jesus can offer us rock-like security for now and Eternity, when we trust in Him and His work of restoring our relationship with God.

Maybe we, like David in Psalm 40 verse 1-2 are in a slimy pit of a different kind. One of despair, or suffering or grief, or trouble which threatens to overwhelm us, despite our trust in God. We are sinking as surely as Shiva was, but she and David cried out – I heard her cry and the Lord will hear ours – even if it is only a whimper. He will lift us out of the mire and set our feet on a firm place – His are mighty, Everlasting Arms which won't fail us.

I'VE STARTED, SO I'LL FINISH

Having just won the Booby Prize for the latest MAFF Lambing Course, any confidence in my future role as a Sheepy Midwife had completely evaporated. The whole experience had been a shock to my system and I had stumbled through the day, trying hard to take everything in.

It had been a well-run affair – with a theory session and then a practical test. And this is where I'd gone completely to pieces.

The vet in charge of our instruction had acquired a couple of dead lambs and a ewe's pelvis to give us real hands-on contact. But coming face to face with death like this before we'd even got any births came as a shock. I'd seen and helped at my cow's calvings and there had never been any loss of life, so I'd been optimistically assuming that things would be the same with my sheep. If only I'd known what I know now!! Death is a fact of life (if I can say that) for a shepherd and I would soon have to come to terms with it. But here was the vet waving two large and perfect looking lambs about which had obviously died at birth. Why? How? And why did the ewe die? My mind was so blown that I missed the crucial introduction to that part of the course.

The birth of a lamb was to be simulated using a large sink of soapy water, in which the ewe's pelvis was fastened. Through this one of the lambs was mal-presented and we students had to reach in as we would when helping a live sheep and try to find out what was wrong. We couldn't see the lamb down in the water, so it was all done by feel, as it would be in reality. We then had to say what was wrong and how we'd sort out the problem and attempt to do it. The pelvis was very narrow, so the smaller your hand the easier it was. Theoretically, therefore, all us women pupils had to be better than the men. But I panicked each time it was my turn and just made uninspired guesses and got everything wrong – but at least I got a feel for the real thing. One remark made by the vet as an aside completely floored me. "Of course," he said, "you all know how to tell the difference between a back and front leg don't you!" Much laughter

37

greeted this, while I daren't say I hadn't got a clue. However, I did take to heart the most emphatic point he then made. "Once you've started you've <u>got</u> to finish!" For the ewe's sake you cannot give up, for unlike cattle she is quickly exhausted and unlike calves the lambs will soon die during any great struggles. In other words there often isn't time for a shepherd to get any other help and he/she must get on with things as quickly as possible.

As I drove home, I wondered however I was going to manage the 50 ewes which I now owned. Up until that year I had seen very few problems in my much smaller flock and had only needed to call the vet once. But now that my husband had been forced to take early retirement, and the farm had to provide an adequate income, vet's bills must be avoided at all costs and I would have to cope on my own. Thirty of the ewes were still relative strangers to me, as they'd only arrived on the farm a short while before. I'd seen them tupped by the ram, since the crayon he wore had marked their fleeces. Each day I had noted any newly-coloured rumps but I had difficulty telling them apart. To the uninitiated sheep all look the same, except for coloured fleeces, but us shepherds get to know their faces, their voices, their walk, and their characters but it takes <u>time.</u> So I wasn't really sure when many would actually lamb. I was also going to face another problem which until I reached in through the narrow pelvis in that sink hadn't occurred to me. It had been so tight I'd barely been able to get my hand through. Now a third of our new flock were ewe lambs, about to lamb for the first time and would be <u>very</u> tight inside and they would panic along with me.

(Had I also known that the bought-in ewes were carrying the vibrionic abortion virus, I think I might have tried leaving the country!)

Mid-February approached and my apprehension increased as I waited for the first lambs, due appropriately on the 14th. Right on cue the 'Horrible Hefferlump' (with apologies to Piglet) triumphantly produced a ghastly-looking set of triplets. At least, she'd done it unaided and loved them dearly. The next day a fine set of twins arrived while I was having breakfast, but after that things took a turn for the worse. Boss Ewe got a set of triplets completely stuck and required a midwife. If only it had been any ewe but her! I loved her so and was very fearful of hurting or harming her! My examination confirmed my worst fears – I opted out, reached for the phone and my cheque book and rang the vet. This good man was to do me a real favour. Knowing us well, he first delivered a severe lecture: "You can't go on calling me Jenny, you won't make any profit! You've <u>got</u> to cope on your own because I <u>won't</u> come out! Then as he sorted out and successfully delivered the lambs, he carefully explained what he was doing and why and how. And this was the turning point – I dared not phone him again. The next problems were also relatively simple to solve and even my feeble gropings succeeded.

When the bought-in ewes began to lamb, the abortions also began and I had to take lamb losses in my stride. There were, in fact, comparatively few but the virus interfered with and held up some of the full-term births and many lambs were weak and needed a lot of care. The whole experience though unwelcome was invaluable and two particular lambings greatly strengthened my midwifery resolves.

The first occurred at 3am - agonised bleatings greeted my visit to the sheep shed and I knew the voice well. It was little Julianna, a ewe lamb I had bottle-reared. Rousing Mike from bed, we set off to her aid. He had to hold her steady, while I attended to her problems. This sounds straightforward enough, but Mike was like the living-dead if awoken in the middle of the night – a walking zombie who had to be talked through everything and frequently shaken awake. But to get back to Julianna. Her lamb was very large and she was very small. As I began to help her, her yells of pain grew louder (most sheep I'm glad to say are silent and stoic in pain) and I nearly freaked out. After much greasing of the lamb's head and shoulders and pulling while she strained, he finally arrived none the worse for the struggle. What kept me going was the MAFF vet's words: "Once you've started you can't give up!" That lambing was a mental triumph of perseverance for me because my resolve had been very near to crumbling more than once, during the battle.

The other lambing which really gave me confidence concerned a ewe known to me as Little 16, and her set of triplets. I found her obviously lambing but the virus was holding things up. Eventually when I examined her, there, deep inside, was just a tail and a head coming together. Now even I knew that couldn't be right. I also knew my first instinct, which was to bring out the lamb whose head I had, wasn't right either. I would need more room to get the front legs to accompany that head and I might get the wrong ones. It would be easier and more certain to find the back legs belonging to the tail. The lamb needed drawing quickly by coming the more risky way, but it was alive and well. I then delivered the other two babies and achieved what the MAFF vet must have thought would be impossible. I'd started, got it right, and finished.

As with every lambing, once the ewe and I were successful both of us then had to continue our work in the lambs, nurturing them to full maturity. And all of this parallels the thoughts Paul expressed in

Philippians 1.6 and 2 Corinthians 5.17 – "If anyone is in Christ he is a new creation" – i.e. if we've committed our lives into His hands we start life anew as Christians.

The 'lambing' is over but that's not the end of the matter because by God's grace we then need developing and nurturing to spiritual maturity. This "good work" He <u>will</u> "complete", as we find in Philippians 1.6. God won't give up on us – He's started His work in us and He'll finish it, and see it through.

Paul was "confident of this" – totally assured and certain of God's thorough workmanship. What a comfort for any of us who despair of ever "being transformed into our Lord's likeness", as we see ourselves letting him down day by day. Our own efforts will fail but God is not relying on them, He's got the work in hand Himself. Our job is to put our lives completely in His care and under His will and direction. There's no thought of failure in God's mind – remember He can and will finish His work in us. So do we just sit back and do nothing? Does a lamb do this? No! He eats; first milk then all the best grazing he can find. He also accepts his mother's guidance and my care and handling. Sometimes life will be painful and puzzling as he faces trials like fly strike or illness and then has to cope with the remedies forced on him. He won't understand, but he will accept the work done in him. If he wanders, he will have to accept my discipline and even if he refuses to co-operate and tries to hinder my work I shan't give him up. I love him too much for that. If we're doubting God's love and care and work in us, at this time, we've only got to turn our eyes on Calvary and "see how He loved!" John 11.36.

CHEW IT OVER (& OVER) (& OVER)

If there's any of you who are not on very good terms with your stomach you will have some sympathy with a cow's (or sheep's) gastric troubles. And if you think you've got problems, just imagine having **FOUR** recalcitrant tummies instead of just one! Your digestion is simplicity itself in comparison – at least, as far as you are concerned. You choose your menu, munch your way through it and that's that. And hopefully your insides then quietly attend to the rest, while you get on with your life.

In complete contrast, a cow's (or sheep's) whole life has to revolve <u>around</u> its digestive system, and that is the way she has to make her living. And even at the risk of making you feel more queasy than you were before you started reading this, I shall have to give you a biology lesson.

First of all, you need a diagram – draw a large rectangle; add a triangle to one end for a head, and tack a tail on the other, and underneath put 2 sticks at each end for the legs. Now you've got your cow; next shade in one third of the rectangle behind the front end and label – **THE RUMEN.** Then divide the rest into 3, labelling these parts as – **OTHER THREE STOMACHS.** And that's about it. A cow does have the odd heart, lung, kidney, womb etc. squeezed in here and there, but in her mind they are fairly unimportant. It is the rumen that rules her life and hence she is a ruminant (as is a sheep, goat, etc. (but <u>not</u> a horse). And as this huge organ in so vital to her, I shall have to concentrate on it in our lesson. I want you to think of it as a mobile and living compost heap because that really sums up its whole purpose. it demands to be stuffed full at very frequent intervals and drives the cow/sheep on to practise a 'sea food' diet (i.e. see food and eat it). So she has to spend up to a couple of hours grazing (for starters). She eats hastily, tugging off great mouthfuls which are gulped down virtually unchewed. This gannet-like behaviour has a 'survival' purpose, because all the time she crops the grass, her specially designed eyes (with rectangular-shaped pupils which give almost 360 degrees vision) watch for predators. I know, I know, you've not seen many lions wandering about East Anglia, but <u>she</u> doesn't know that!

41

When she has crammed in as much as she can, she seeks a place of 'safety' so that she can lie down and deal with all this food properly. This is just like the sheep who is speaking in Psalm 23, who says of the Lord her Shepherd; "He makes me lie down in green pastures.' Notice it is not what we would expect – we would have thought the sheep or cow would say: "He makes me graze in green pastures." A sheep who is so vulnerable and defenceless does have many enemies even here in Norfolk – just the sight of a dog is enough to give her a heart attack. So if a ewe is to lie down things must be super safe – hence this lovely picture of complete security in the Lord.

Once the cow (sheep) is at rest, she can get on with her meal. This involves her in regurgitating boluses of the partially fermented grass from her rumen. Each of these mouthfuls is then very thoroughly chewed around 50 times (as her mummy taught her), then swallowed down for the digestion to continue and be completed in the rest of the compound stomach. More and more is burped up and slowly and carefully gone over, through a period of about an hour for a cow. She grazes then cuds meditatively in this pattern about 6 times through the 24 hours. (She doesn't need 8 hours beauty sleep like us, and only cat naps for a while after her cudding). For us cowhands and shepherds there is nothing more reassuring than to see our herds at rest and contentedly chewing. It's a sure sign of health and well-being. (It is not a sign of rain as the 'old wives' have it, by the way!)

The steady rhythmical movement of those bovine jaws has a most calming effect if you spend time with your cattle at such a time. It is a real therapy for stress and anxiety. However, a rise in a farmer's blood pressure is guaranteed if any member of the herd is discovered not eating and worse still not cudding. And if a check on her rumen reveals that it has stopped working, and all that can be heard is a deathly silence, this is a signal for an outbreak of Farmer's Panic. How do we know the rumen is in stasis (stoppage)? We press our ear against the animal's left side, and listen. If all is well, the contents of this stomach should turn over once every minute or so, with a satisfying 'urble burble'. But if the 'compost heap' is lying inert and leaden, you've got to find out **WHY and DO SOMETHING!**

Young stock, especially calves, who, although suckling for months, begin grazing a few days after birth, are particularly prone to gastric upsets. This is because the flora (bacteria) of the rumen, which have begun to multiply and build up once the baby has deliberately licked up some soil, is very delicate and easily interrupted in its development. I wish I could say that a Rennie or the like could be a solution. A cure is difficult and complicated and sometimes only time can be a healer.

Liquid paraffin, Epsom salts, or special rumen activators can be tried – all in a drench, but it's not easy to administer, I can tell you.

More rarely a <u>cow's</u> digestion can go to pieces as a result of some other underlying cause, like Acetonaemia for example. The only bad case of this that I've ever seen, was in Cherry, a cousin of another Dexter, May, who I still own. Cherry calved one February producing a fine boy who I named Jasper Carrot. All was well with him, but not with her. The familiar and unmistakable smell of nail varnish (acetone) seemed to fill the cowshed the day following his birth. Mother's whole system had been too stressed and Ketosis set in. She lost all interest in food, just when she desperately needed to eat well, to produce the milk for her baby. (He soon needed at least 2 gallons a day.) Despite cortisone injections and other treatments she grew thinner and weaker and nothing tempted her appetite. Fresh grass and exercise are the best cures – both in short supply in winter! So I had to resort to leading her about on a rope, especially along the lane verges where grass always grows earlier than on the fields. I did this regularly for weeks, and also found her really delicious titbits like bread, cakes, fruit, and vegetable scraps. But only the eventual Spring flush of growth in April, got her eating and cudding healthily again.

Well, here ends my lesson on a cow's digestion and I think it's time I gave someone like Coral (another Dexter) a special spot in the curriculum, so she can teach us all some home truths. Since meditation (a word derived from rumination) is so central to her every day, she is a perfect illustration of David's words in Psalm 119.97 "I mediate on Your law all day long"! Mind you I can't vouch for the depth of thought that goes on behind her soft, brown eyes. But I'm sure that the winter cuds of hay make her dream of summer meadows and sweet clover. At any rate, the main point she would want to make is, that just as she is so careful over digesting her food, we need to "read, mark, learn and inwardly digest" God's word. We are not therefore expected to meditate in the vacuous way advocated by some Eastern philosophies; that idea would be laughable to any cow! She wouldn't be found chewing over nothing! No! she would find all the most nourishing food she possibly could that would build her up to her fullest potential, for her sake and her calf's. I'm sure too that Coral would suggest that since she must 'Cud or Die', this could be a good motto for us as well. Her advice might go something like this: "Look, I'm prepared to spend at least 12 hours a day grazing and cudding just to keep me alive on this earth. Surely you can give up time to chew over your Daily Bread for Eternity." John 6.27.

WELL-TIMED

Clocks and watches simply can't cope with me – I seem to jinx them into doing silly things or just seizing up altogether. Take the only consistent time-piece I've ever owned as an example – it is an electric kitchen clock which has manfully struggled on despite the continual blips in our current. However it has developed a sort of nervous tic (sorry about the pun) and resolutely goes <u>backwards</u> after even the most minor of breaks in the power. This habit has resulted in much confusion amongst visitors.

I was once the proud owner of an expensive sailing/diving watch, which I took on my solo trips on the near-by estuary. It was waterproof down to 100 metre depths – however I rather hoped never to have to test that claim! I doubted it anyhow, because one summer a barley bug (a minute thrip) managed to get into the face, so the time was permanently set at 1 bug past 3 o'clock! The farm spells death for watches – the vibrations from the physical activity are fatal for most designs. And none of them like flying off my wrist and landing in cow pats! So, I never wear one now preferring to trust in the built in clock I seem to have. It is linked to tummy time and to a definite feeling I have for every minute that passes.

Although our Eternal God is outside time in one sense, He is also <u>very</u> concerned and involved with time. Our Bibles are full of exact times, days, dates and years – these matter to Him and are all in His plans. Much more than that, His timing is impeccable and when He entered time and sent His Son to us, that event was in His plans to the last detail. No other time in history would have done. But His plans reach down to our lives, "Our times are in His hand" Psalm 139.2 and even before we were born He was with us, "knitting us together in our mother's wombs" V.13. This brings His involvement with time, right to our doorsteps and right to every minute that ticks by.

Three years ago a sequence of such finely-timed events occurred here which only God could have organised. At that point, I owned about a quarter of the original farm, the rest of the land (three fields) having been bought by two other neighbouring farmers. My 33 acre holding was therefore sandwiched between megafarms which are basically vast estates and these are always on the look-out for expansion and the eradication of any small concerns.

Out of the blue (to my eyes but not in God's of course!) the two large Station Farm fields on my side of the lane came back on the market! Big farmers very seldom sell, so it was a surprising move. One of these fields shared a half mile boundary with my main 25 acre pasture and could easily be accessed from my land. The terrible droughts had meant I was always short of grazing, so it would be very useful. Should I take any action? More to the point could I take any action? And above all what was God's will? In the next days as I began to lay it all out before Him, I went off to a Bible Study and discovered we were studying Joshua and Achsah's request for a field (Jos. 15. 17-19) and her blessing.... Just a co-incidence? No! all such are God-incidences, but I didn't want to let my hopes rise because the Conditions of Sale were really prohibitive for me. The main ones refused a bid for only one of the fields – joint bids were expected. I could not afford the whole 70 acres and knew of no-one who would wish or be able to partner me. So even though God seemed to be saying I should take action, I really could not do much. I decided to put in a bid for the field bordering my land even though I knew it was unacceptable. At least it showed my interest and willingness to co-operate with anyone wanting the other piece of land. (Although the chances of that were very slim indeed.) Two of my neighbours had already shown interest in the whole acreage and submitted sealed bids. Anyway, I had peace of mind, because I had done all I could and had to leave the result totally in God's hands, knowing "nothing is too hard for the Lord", Gen. 18.14. I also prayed for the strength to really accept whatever outcome, even though I'd be disappointed should I lose the field.

Now, if all this had come up nine months earlier the whole thing would have been academic, since I was not financially in a position to buy anything on this scale. But an uncle of mine had just left me an inheritance, so God had arranged the right year. He had also been doing the same thing in the lives of two other people who I had yet to meet; so that their plans for a cider orchard to replace their previous occupation were coming to a climax.

It will be necessary to give exact days and dates from now on because God was to take our times in His hand in specific detail. A week after placing my bid with the land agent, I was amazed ("O you of little faith") Matthew 6.30, to find a message on my answer phone from him, to say that there <u>was</u> someone who wanted to purchase just the other field alone and would I agree to meet him. And it was critical we did see each other quickly as we only had 10 days before July 4th, the closing date for tenders. So, on Sunday June 26th he and his partner came over to the farm. But my hopes were not to be raised too high, since they were in fact much more interested in a piece of land nearer their home. They had bid for it and were to hear the next Friday, July 1st, whether or not they had been successful. I was powerless to act, and wonderfully thrown into God's care completely again. And He gave me a reassurance on July 1st from the reading I was following for that day from Deut. Chapter 1. "See I have given you this land". I did not want to delude myself, but this seemed plain enough even for me. Early on the Saturday morning of July 2nd I found another message left for me, this time from my partners. They had lost the other land, despite their optimism, and despite a very high bid. So we met that evening to consider our position and to work out what we could afford to offer. For them, the other field was 10 acres too much, but I had a friend who I knew would love to own that amount if he could be persuaded to buy it just at that time.

We left the final decision until the next day July 3rd after I had taken my friend sailing. By 5pm he'd agreed to join us and we all had one final meeting to drew up our tender, seal it and begin wondering if it would be high enough to cap the agricultural giants' bids which were already in. I was to deliver our tender before noon the next day (the final deadline) – July 4th. Owing to pressure of farm work I made it to the agents by 11am with just an hour to spare. I seemed to catch them off guard; I suppose they'd never imagine anyone would leave it so late. I was told "we'd hear very soon if we were not in the running", and as I mused on that while driving home, I realised what a very slender chance we had against men of limitless funds. We had no hope in either theirs or the agent's eyes.

Within an hour the phone had rung, and I'd been asked if we had money to meet the bid – such an enquiry meant the bids were close. Since we had, the next call within another hour, clinched the matter – our bid had been accepted!

My local farming friends were speechless with disbelief on learning the result; God had taken on giants for us, quite as big as Og, and of course one of my set readings for July 5th was Deuteronomy Chapter 3! (in verse 11, Og's enormous bed's measurements show how huge he was!)

If you're thinking that God cannot possibly be interested in all the sort of dates and times I've recounted (and you may even feel it is too arrogant to imagine He's bothered about us as individuals in this way), I suggest we go back to Psalm 139 – From beginning to end David is sure that God has a full and final knowledge of his life V.1.2 "..You know me, You know when I sit down and when I rise" V.16. "All the days ordained for me were written in your book before one of them came to be". V.5 "You hem me in – behind and before". God loves and cares like that about us all because He made us and has plans for each one of us.

And He is concerned about dates in a big way – just take the Flood account as an example. There was no need as far as we're concerned for such accuracy – Genesis 7.11. for example – "in the 600th year of Noah's life, on the 17th day of the 2nd month – on that day the floodgates of heaven were opened". Genesis 8.13. "By the 27th day of the 2nd month the earth was completely dry".

If days matter so much to God how much more should our own matter to us. Every one is precious, and not to be wasted; "Lord teach us to number our days aright, so that we gain a heart of wisdom" - Psalm 90.12.

KATIE ET AL

Through the six months of winter my daily life follows a fairly set pattern. It revolves around the cows' needs, which take up all my time during the shortest days. From dawn to dusk, I feed, muck out, bed down, feed again and put to bed all the 30 or so cattle. I am the complete cowsbody, since I'm chiefly a waitress and lavatory attendant (strictly in

that order!) I am at their beck and call and woe betide me if I am late for any meal time. I have to remember these diners have no patience and no manners and will never give me any tips!

The routine is a relentless grind but I accept this as part of their care and because I love them. It is, I have to admit, rather dull but very good therapy in troubled times. It certainly kept me sane during Michael's terrible illness since I <u>had</u> to get on with the work and my thoughts were channelled into the task on hand.

Such an ordered life also affords a kind of peace in its purpose. And you certainly don't need one of those little electronic personal organisers which are the thing to own at the moment. The cows have it all worked out for you and won't let you forget <u>anything</u>! So it is very easy for me to be lulled into a false sense of security hardly having to think for myself at all. I <u>know</u> what each day holds in store and can go around in a sort of clockwork or robotic trance. But this kind of thinking is soon upturned when you live with animals, and as Proverbs 27.1 points out: "Do not boast about tomorrow for you do not know what a day may bring forth".

Many a lambing or calving has 'brought forth' a few shocks for me during one of these so-called 'predictable' days. The weather too can interrupt and add its own problems to the usual run of events. An over-night blizzard can cause complete chaos as happened one winter, cutting us off for a week, and even taking <u>two</u> of us just to push a wheelbarrow through the snow.

Last January a bitterly cold snap gave me much extra work and worry because the whole farm (yards, tracks, little field) became a skating rink! Neither the cows nor I are Torvils or Deans and I spent the days praying that none of us would slip and break something. (The outlook, by the way, for a cow if she does break a limb is usually humane slaughter.) Then I had a rare brainwave. I decided to scatter ashes on the most lethal areas, only to find these so terrified many of the cattle that they skittered round them, slipping and sliding even worse than ever! After a fortnight during which the ice became more and more hard packed and dangerous, a thaw arrived. I almost began to miss the excitement of balancing a loaded barrow on the ice and using it as a sort of Skidoo-cum-Zimmer frame.

Still at last we had terra (albeit very muddy) firma and we were back to the old routine and dulling of our senses. Thus relaxed I was caught unaware by the Day of the Bombshells.

Steel and I were gaily setting off to the farm to let the cows out for breakfast when we paused... whatever was that funny noise? It was a cross between a loud deep moaning and heavy snoring, and it had to be bovine. Hurrying to the cow yard gate I could see where it was coming from. For, huddled by a wall, was Katie, shuddering in time with the row she was making. Every breath was obviously agony and she could barely move. She did eventually painfully stagger out with the others, grunting and groaning at each step. She would not, of course, eat and was in too much pain even to lie down. I desperately tried to think what was wrong with her. Pneumonia? No – too sudden an onset. She'd been fine at tea-time last night.

A wire or obstruction in her stomach? Nooo.... too sudden again surely.

Had she slipped and strained herself on the ice remnants? Perhaps...

Or had Rupert, (a bullock with a pair of really nasty horns) attacked her? Perhaps... She was big and bossy and good at picking a fight.

I trailed off to phone the vet but since I couldn't give him any definite symptoms he saw no point in coming out, suggesting instead some pain killers.

Going back to the farm I became convinced her problem was definitely mechanical, as she couldn't bear anyone near her. She stood alone, away from any hassle and I felt time would be the healer if only she could keep quiet.

Well I had to get on. The sheep needed letting out and breakfast so I went off to their building. As I began opening their hurdle I spotted a brown yearling ewe-lamb lying by the feeder. She wasn't stirring as all the others came to greet me and when I reached her, I found she'd dropped dead overnight. She'd been fine at tea-time but if this was Pulpy Kidney (the most likely cause of death) it can kill in a few hours. The bacteria multiply in their millions in such a short time that total septicaemia sets in, and there is no cure. Stress of the cold weather may have triggered it off. My despair was heightened by the thought of trying to dig a grave for her in the still frozen ground.

When I got round to the chickens who are free to roam, live in the barn and are given wheat day and night to top up their own pickings, you've probably guessed I was in for a nasty surprise. Two or three seemed bad on their legs and not interested in food! They are normally very healthy, since they lead such an outdoor life-style, but wild birds were carrying a new kind of fowl-pest about and this was the beginning of a mini-epidemic which killed 6 of the hens in the end.

At this point I began to wish I'd stayed in bed! It would have been quite nice to have missed this day out altogether, especially when I found I had to bucket 60 gallons of water into the cows' tank, because I hadn't protected the taps overnight (the thaw had made me lax). So once I was back indoors with the daylight over, I was feeling decidedly weak at the knees. And my self-confidence was at a low ebb after such an illustration of those words in Proverbs I quoted earlier. Neither man (nor woman) is in control of <u>one</u> day, let alone his/her destiny.

As I took stock of all I had encountered through those daylight hours, and of which I would have preferred to steer clear, I remembered David's words in Psalm 118.24. "This is the day the Lord has made, we will rejoice and be glad in it." Hmmm. Well, I hadn't exactly done that! It's easy to rejoice on a nice, sunny blissful day (I thought) but not on a bad one. Still... David praised the Lord at all times as the Psalms show so well – in fact, his praises rang out louder as his experiences got darker. So did Paul's and he put this thought even more strongly, in Philippians 4.4, exhorting us to "Rejoice in the Lord, <u>always</u>". How ever can I (or you) do this? The clue is "<u>in the Lord</u>" – we can't naturally and in our own power do so, but there are those tremendous words in Nehemiah 8.10 – "the joy of the Lord is your strength". Jesus' joy is unchanging, it is ours for the asking. Jesus Christ the same yesterday, today and forever.

FEE, FI, FO, FUM...

Poor Miss Muppet was scared off by a spider and if it was one of those great big hairy sorts I don't blame her! But if it was only a small one, she was a bit silly, and she certainly wouldn't have liked to know that apparently there are a million spiders in an acre of ground. That means that there are plenty round here and most of the big long-legged ones seem to make for my bath. Because Arachnophobia is shared by so many of us, we can sympathise with such a fear, even if it is irrational as far as the species of spider encountered in the U.K. are concerned. But we don't stop to analyse the things that really put us in a funk even if our minds <u>are</u> fooling us.

Sheep and cattle don't either. They run first and then stop and think a lot later. I've already dealt with ewes' and lambs' panic buttons in other yarns, so I'll use a bovine example for a change. It was towards the end of last winter when I'd got to the stage of running out of cows' roots (beet and parsnips). So I was scratching about trying to find something else for their teas which could be added to the basic menu of hay and straw. I decided to cut any greenery I could find around the farm – delectable weeds, lawn mowings and scythings. I then had the brainwave of adding some pulp nuts to these bits. Pulp nuts are neither pulpy nor nuts; they are pellets of pressed beet remnants after the sugar (for us) has been extracted. They are very palatable, and sweet and full of energy and the sheep adore them. The cows would need about 2½ cwt a week so having duly bought in several sacks, I reached the evening when I could lovingly put their ration out ready for their homecoming. And once I'd opened the gates and brought them up, I dashed into the yard to watch how they would enjoy their treat.

The youngsters were the first to arrive and having taken one look in the bins they panicked! As all the older cattle followed in, mass hysteria broke out as everyone dashed to and fro, hoping to find a bin of food without any of **THE THINGS** in them. "Ah!" I thought as I saw Folly lumbering in, "She'll <u>love</u> the nuts, I know". On reaching her bin she stopped in horror, then quickly backed away crashing into the others who were skittering around. There was utter chaos and consternation as they all tried to escape from the **NASTIES** and try and find something they could eat. Just think of it! Folly, a three-quarter ton giant petrified of a beet pellet ½" long! I crept out of the yard, shut their gate to and went up to the house in despair. This had been consumer resistance taken to a ridiculous extreme. I actually think that one or two might have eaten some of the pulp if it hadn't been for the daft reaction of all the others who put them off.

Fear is as infectious as any virus and April's story highlights this even further. Brothercross April, a pedigree Dexter, is now 10 years old but I am going back to when she was a young maiden heifer of 18 months or so. A friend who had come to see our herd, fell in love with the cows and wanted to own a young one. Only April fitted the bill, but she had hardly been haltered at all, although she did know her name. Like all her breed, she was easily ruffled and not at all stolid like a Charolais usually is. Tracey, my friend had seen how tame the likes of Honey and Folly etc. were, and hoped as I did that April would soon become as handleable and would respond as Tui had done (see `Designer Training). But of course, any animal moving to a new home is always very unsettled and easily scared and she would need kid-glove handling.

I suggested April would be best housed and then tethered in the day (as I had Tui at first), so she got to know her surroundings and Tracey too. She was also going to be lonely and needed a lot of human reassurance. But sadly for both April and Tracey, things didn't go well. And after a week I had a phone call asking for help. Mike and I went over and we found April in her shed and reluctant to come out.

I decided to put her onto a halter and lead her out to her tether and as everyone watched I went in to her. It was then that great waves of fear began to wash over me and they were coming from both the group of people outside the door and from April. I was caught in the middle of these really tense vibes and the atmosphere was so electric I could hardly believe it. I was being infected by everybody's fears too and I had to speak severely to myself. "Oh! Come on Jenny" I thought, "this is only April your little heifer. Whatever are you scared of?!"

I gently coaxed a rope on her and led her out and all seemed okay when we left some time later. But by the next evening poor Tracey was urgently ringing me again. April had panicked and injured herself on the tether chain. We set off to help at once, this time with the livestock trailer to fetch her home as Tracey felt that was best.

We found everyone in distress and we agreed that we should have April back. Tracey came home with us too, and saw April unloaded and put in the yard for the night. She joined Folly who had calved that day and had come off the field with baby so I could empty some of her over-pressed udder. As we watched the three of them together, we all got the giggles. The youngster, who I'd named Irving, was already nearly as big as April and definitely had much bigger knees. They were not only huge but very knobbly and kept knocking together in his gangling efforts to get about. He helped to lighten the whole atmosphere and Tracey was quite sure she didn't want to take him home!

So fear is clearly contagious and can soon reach epidemic proportions. Numbers 13 which deals with the spies' report on God's Promised Land, shows that it's not only cows who can hype one another up. That report began to resemble something out of Jack and The Beanstalk as the account of the giants got more and more exaggerated. And the result was a fatal infection of faint-heartedness.

In Isaiah 12.2. we can find a cure – "God is my salvation – and I will trust and not be afraid". Then our king-sized (Deut. 3.11.) trials, difficulties, problems and even dangers will be shrunk down to pulp nut dimensions, as we refuse to lose faith in God's power and promises.

SIT – STAY – WAIT!

Faced with incomprehension and blank looks we British tend to resort to shouting and speaking V E R Y D E L I B E R A T E L Y. Anyone who has lost their sight has probably been yelled at as though they were deaf as well. And once Mike started getting out and about after his laryngectomy (and so could not speak) many people spoke very loudly as they thought he'd become hard of hearing as well! And of course, if we find ourselves in conversation with someone of foreign tongue, we're back to where I started.

Living among my sheep and cattle who neither know nor care about 'Sotto Voce', I could perhaps be forgiven for shouting all day on the farm. But, in fact, their noise somehow reduces me to a whisper, so I seldom raise my voice to them, except in dire circumstances. And they actually respond best to being softly spoken to, especially as they have to shut up in order to hear me.

However, large and boisterous dogs have the opposite effect on me and Steel has been no exception. In his manic enthusiasm nothing seems to cut any ice unless I go puce and bellow! Having attended dog training classes I've found I'm not alone – the noise generated by exasperated owners is unbelievable! If you watch 'One Man and His Dog', who work with much distance between them, a loud voice and whistle are vital assets and without them the shepherd might as well herd the sheep himself.

From the day I brought Steel home as a 10 week old, I had to be firm in all I said to him. He came with his own ideas about things and his intelligence was matched by perseverance and a very strong will. If I was going to be in some sort of command, I'd got to be more determined than him and say what I meant with authority. I also had to mean what I said – so the commands had to be ones which were to be obeyed – always and preferably instantly. So **NO – LEAVE** for example, meant leave alone, at once – i.e. leave (don't touch) the electric fence – he soon learnt that one! Or leave the cat's food at once, not after he'd gobbled it up; leave that ewe before she got badly frightened, and leave that cow and calf before the mother tries to kill you. One afternoon "**NO WAIT!**" saved his life as he ran ahead of me to cross our lane and I only heard a car at the last moment.

I can well remember wanting to teach him **NO-DOWN!** As a youngster, when he greeted people. I tried to enlist the aid of a couple of friends who he particularly loves, by asking them to tell him the command as he bounded up. But their kindly gentle voices had no effect whatsoever. He didn't think they meant what they said. So for an order to be given to a dog successfully it must be loud and clear – i.e. plain and simple to understand, just two words are ideal. You must also be consistent in your issuing of them and in your expectation of a correct response. Then the dog knows where he is. His name is also better if it is short and easy to say, especially in emergencies. (A rule I've applied to cattle too.) Steel is actually 'Iolanda Venture', in the Kennel Club Records, but by the time I got all that out he would have run into the road or whatever. Worse still, if I had to yell the pedigree name Florushdon of Knotting! instead of May (a cow), I'd be lucky to get it right each time, let alone get any response.

Two of Steel's earliest and very important commands involved waiting on his own and so are actually quite difficult to teach a young pup who for security wants to be with his master, but they were my best successes. I use the word success loosely and friends of Steel will understand why! The first was **SIT-STAY!** as Steel came to me one November in the midst of calving and then lambing, and he had to learn to sit patiently while I helped at any birth. One particular morning a ewe was having a very difficult time and I was well over an hour with the sheep before I remembered that I'd left little Steel 'sat-staying'. I rushed back to the gate to find him huddled in a bit of shelter, but still quietly sitting. At that time, part of the farm was unfenced and he could so easily have pottered off. It was a lesson well-learnt and has meant he will sit for even longer times now.

The other command is **SIT-WAIT!** Issued when I need Steel to be especially still in the face of some kind of dramatic event (like the cows making mayhem) and I've got to sort things out without his 'help'. Often I tack the two orders together **SIT STAY WAIT!** If you only knew Steel you could imagine that such requirements test his obedience and self-control to the limits, since he is hyper-active (I fear his mother must have laced his milk with orange squash!) I can sympathise with him because where he is **ACTION MAN/DOG**, I'm **ACTION WOMAN**. I actually do expect Rome to be built in a day, so

Sit Wait is nearly as difficult for me as it is for Steel. Like him, I want to be up and off, almost too impatient to wait for instructions.

Steel's father is a Champion Police Dog and this means he really knows how to trust and obey. Sit, Stay, Wait! means just that – for hours if need be and in the face of testing situations which may make him fret and be anxious. But he will <u>not</u> make a move. He and his son (in a much lesser way!) highlight what God asks us to do – Psalm 37.7: "Be still before the Lord, wait patiently for Him and do not fret...."

First, we are to 'be still' i.e. sit down and be quiet and listen, like Steel and the cows, so the noise of our strivings or distress does not drown out "God's still, small voice" 1 Kings 19.12. Then, even if things seem, to us, to be getting out of control, to 'wait patiently' and <u>not</u> take matters into our own hands. God knows best and His timing is perfect (as I was to learn in 'Well-Timed'- another tale). We may also need to adjust to God's rhythm and remember that once He acts, we'll often find it very difficult to keep up.

TIPPEX

Crystal is a Red Dexter cow that I helped to bring into the world 14 years ago. She was named after a gemstone (as this is my method for all the pedigree herd members) and it was the C year for Herd Book registrations. But the name fits her perfectly, if you consider that crystalline action is based on coagulation – i.e. forming a clot, because sadly she is such a duffer!

She was born weak in the knees (for a time they worked back to front!) and weak in the head and heart; so she lacks courage and is over-fastidious and excitable. Her failing reminds me of those words in Isaiah 35.3:

"Strengthen the feeble hands, steady the knees that give way, say to those with fearful hearts – be strong and do not fear".

I seem to have been saying this to Crystal all her life. And this is well-illustrated by her reaction to planes (or worse still helicopters). Most of the herd react mildly to noisy low-flying, but Crystal goes berserk. She is always the first to spot the aircraft and behaves as though it is about to get her, like some kind of Terradactyl! Her panic naturally infects others who then run around in a flat spin endangering themselves and my fences.

Of course if any one of the cows is in trouble, it is usually Crystal or one of her offspring, so I really shouldn't have been surprised when she collapsed in the middle of her third calving. She had appeared to be well on the way to giving birth at 9am but things had gone very slowly and I had pottered off to get some lunch. On my return I found her all of a heap, with the calf's feet well out. She'd gone into a coma and it had to be milk fever. A half-mile dash, with hurdling over the electric fences thrown in, got me to the phone. I needed the vet, calcium and a flutter valve quickly. Hypocalcaemia usually comes on after calving but Crystal had to be different. It is also associated by stress – stress of pregnancy and milk production, and as the udder distends. The condition may therefore occur in heavy yielders (particularly in a dairy herd). Now Crystal's udder is not large by any means, it is just about adequate for baby with little or none to spare, so she was not an obvious milk-fever candidate. But she was good at hyping herself up over anything and she had also chosen a 90 degree F. heatwave for the event. The strain of such high temperatures and dehydration had probably been the last straw, and of course, Crystal's red coat makes her less able to cope with extremes of weather for some reason.

Between us all, the vet, me, Michael (and even Crystal in the end) a healthy live calf eventually arrived. The calcium once given intravenously works just like magic and within a quarter of an hour Crystal was up, and although very tottery and unable to strain, did her best to co-operate while we carefully pulled baby out.

Since then she's repeated the trick again, although I caught her before she went unconscious, so that the calcium and her own efforts produced the infant that time. If however, she calves in the autumn or winter when it is cooler, she seems able to avoid the problem. Still, I can never guarantee this and she always keeps me on my toes. So last year was no different, especially as she was very slow and I spent some hours checking and watching and waiting until a fine bull calf arrived.

Perhaps I should have guessed this was too good to be true and not have been so puzzled as I was during the next few days. When I checked mother and child the following morning all did not seem quite right. She was lowing a great deal and baby didn't seem to be sucking. Did she have mastitis? Nooo, but maybe one or two quarters were dud... I decided to top baby up with a bottle now and then. By day 5, the weather had deteriorated – it was nearly November – the calf seemed poorly and forever dribbling when I fed him. Had he now got the Farm Bug? This is a stomach one, which can kill if not treated. I decided to pull all the herd in at nights from then on, for his sake. And this would also be my opportunity to eartag him (a legal requirement) and ring him (as I didn't want him to be a bull). It was then I discovered he was not entire and didn't need ringing. This was the first calf I had ever known to be malformed in such a way.

Then I noticed that as he sucked on a teat, the milk kept dribbling back down his nostrils, (I was later to discover he had a cleft palate). He was also incapable of holding Mum's teat for any length of time, despite her patience. This was partly due to the fact that he held his head at a funny angle. Slowly light dawned – this calf was physically and mentally handicapped or as a dear old vet friend of mine would say "you've got a daft one there, I'm afraid". I really should never have interfered and begun bottle feeding him, but once I'd started, it was hard to withdraw this nourishment and let nature take its course.

It was hard for me and for Crystal, because her bond with him was very strong. For a while, he held his own and I named him "Tippex" as he needed a lot of altering. But after a couple of months he became really poorly, refused even a bottle and faded away.

Crystal was absolutely devastated and mooed day and night almost non-stop. I had to wheel Tippex's body about in an old wheelbarrow – out onto the field in the day, back into the Yard at night, because Crystal would not leave him. Eventually when I had to bury the calf, Crystal became inconsolable – calling to me all the day and watching my every movement in case I was bringing her baby back to her. It was a very harassing time for her and for me. I felt very distressed because she, like us humans, had carried her baby for 9 months, had then become very close to him and I tried hard to comfort her and ease her grief. If you are thinking I'm over-dramatising this, because cows surely can't have feelings as powerful as I've described, I can assure you I am not. I've understated her sorrow and her loneliness and not detailed how she pined and refused to eat. It isn't just us people who have the prerogative in feelings, and grief and suffering, cows, sheep, dogs – well, all animals we really understand – share these emotions and need comfort too.

I did my best to console Crystal because I cared, and Isaiah 63.9 kept coming to my mind. "In all their distress, He too was distressed". Oh! How God cares about our suffering! He's alongside us in them. He weeps with us as Jesus did at Lazarus' death and Mary and Martha's grief. And as Isaiah prophesied in Chapter 53.3 Jesus "was despised and rejected by men, a man of sorrows and familiar with suffering" and he faced all this on the Cross for us and our salvation. Jesus knows all our suffering and pain, He's been there and He is with us in our heartache. He wants to cradle us in His arms and give us comfort, and so he calls to us...

"Come unto Me, all you who are weary and burdened and I will give you rest". Matthew 11.28.

RUBY'S SON

Ruby is Crystal's daughter and her look-alike! Not only that, her temperament is very similar and even more ominously her calving record looks like paralleling her mother's. "Like mother, like daughter" – I've seen this proverb so well-illustrated in cows and sheep families and we can find it quoted in scripture in Ezekiel 16.44.

A month after Tippex's arrival (see previous yarn) Ruby quietly and unaided produced a fine, strong son. She was a proud and caring new parent, if a little nervous, and he grew well. Thus lulled into a false sense of security and pre-occupied with Tippex's problems I was unprepared for the events that were to follow.

It was almost Christmas and I was exceptionally busy and nearly missed the fact that Ruby's son was ailing. (I had not, for some reason, named him – it was the T year and there were plenty of options, but nothing had fitted). I couldn't put a finger on what was wrong with him... You're probably wondering why I didn't call a vet at this point. But it is no good doing so if there are no obvious symptoms – e.g. a raised temperature, diarrhoea, coughing etc. The calf can't tell you anything, so you must work things out.

Soon after, however, his breathing became laboured and he started grinding his teeth (in pain) and now I had something to go on. This was pneumonia and could be treated accordingly – he had to be injected (with difficulty) and fussed over, and he began to respond. But his recovery was not good and I still felt there was an underlying cause, which remained undetected. Darkest, deepest January and February are not good months to be ill and I just hoped he could hang on until the Spring and the new grass. I was especially concerned for him on cold wet days, as the herd are always outside for a few hours and you can't keep one cow and calf in. She would break back and cause chaos as she hates being alone. So I was glad for his sake when it was teatime and I could let them in.

On this never-to-be-forgotten day as I went to their gate, telling Steel to 'Sit Wait' near-by, I was startled to hear a calf's 'silly' moo. (It is a babyish kind of playful roar, the sort that develops into a full throated threat in a full-grown bull or cow). The noise was very close, and as I turned, I saw it was Ruby's son who was throwing himself down and entangling all his legs in the bars of the gate. He was having a fit at an incredibly dreadful moment and place. (In of course, the family tradition!)

The situation was a waking nightmare and I'd better explain why. The 30 or so strong herd were poised to dash off the field for tea, having seen me arrive. To their horror, **A THING** was thrashing about blocking their way, making weird noises and terrifying even stolid souls like Folly. Their gatekeeper wasn't opening up, but lying on the ground with **THE THING** and wrestling with it (I was frantically trying either to extricate the flailing limbs or drag the calf out of the way, but deep oozy mud and his weight were foiling my efforts).

Pressure from herd members at the back forced those in front to take action. Driven by real fear and thoughts of tea, the panic stricken mob charged at the gate; some leaped over, others crashed through, and all those flying hooves, great and small flashed past me, as I tried to duck out of the way. Many times my head and shoulders were struck and I was in very real danger of being badly kicked and trampled underfoot. Fortunately, the heavies of the likes of Folly and Honey held back and once I could scramble to my feet, I managed to force open the remains of the gate and let them through. I suppose it was all over in a minute or two but it seemed much longer. I could scarcely believe I was still in one piece.

At last I was able to really try to attend to Ruby's son. He was in the throes of severe spasms and was totally unaware of his surroundings. He was having a fit of the staggers and it was a hopeless scenario. This illness is where the animal's magnesium reserves suddenly drop to a dangerously low level, because of stress (illness in his case). Even if I had been able to administer magnesium to him in time, his heart was failing and few animals survive such a fit. (You usually just find one has inexplicably dropped dead.) Sheep are often lost in this way, but cattle being constitutionally stronger, are less likely to be victims. As he lay dying, I remembered Steel who I'd left sit staying near the gate! Fortunately, he is disobedient enough to have slunk off and was cowering uninjured in the Barn. (I know of German Shepherd Dogs who would stay in the face of such peril, but I'm glad he has a stronger survival instinct than that.)

Ruby soon realised that her boy wasn't with her and once again I was wheelbarrowing a lifeless calf about, not only that evening, but for a few days. She was as inconsolable as Crystal had been, because her bond had become very strong indeed in three months. She also reacted exactly like her mother when I had to bury him and since she is less close to me, I couldn't console her at all.

Then an amazing thing happened. Ruby and Crystal found solace in each other. You see there are always good family ties between cattle because they feed their calves for 8-9 months. And then the youngsters often stay in the herd until they are 18 months before being sold. And mothers, whose daughters remain here permanently, keep the bond between them alive. So Ruby naturally went to Crystal for love and comfort. The two licked and groomed each other, lay down together, stood side by side, and mooed in unison. They understood and could sympathise with each other's loss. It was a wonderful inter-twining which helped them, as I could never have done.

If these two 'lesser creatures' for whom man is to be a steward can do this for each other, we too, who are in God's image, should at least rise to this. Crystal 'used' her suffering to bring comfort to Ruby in a way only she could. I know that in my very dark times when Mike was terminally ill, I could more readily go to those who'd also been through bad times. "So a Christian's suffering can be wrested into service for others" as Selwyn Hughes put it in his series of daily notes on "Suffering – God is enough", and of course Paul had found this to be so as he wrote to the Corinthians 2 Chapter 1. He assured them that "the God of all comfort comforts us in our troubles, so we can comfort those in any trouble with the comfort we ourselves have received from God".

God is enough for us and His grace can flow out of our suffering to others. Our pain can become a pearl for others to share.

SCUD FOR THE LORD

I'm very glad I share the greater part of my days with sheep and cows, because, they like me, don't mind making fools of themselves. They are totally un-British wearing their hearts on their 'sleeves', and letting their joy freely rip. And if they could see me of an evening 'dancing' away to a wonderful minuet or gavotte by Haydn or Bach or whoever, they would nod approval (and try to join in, I expect). But I am quite aware what my human friends would think!

Now, you have probably heard of the Turkey Trot, but perhaps not of the Cow Caper and the Sheep Scud. You might like to learn them. The steps are not very tricky – you just need to be fairly fit and very enthusiastic. So, I'll describe them in a moment. But first of all I must assure you, if doubts are rising, that sheep and cattle can dance and play like the best of us. Job knew this, in fact God told him "all the wild animals play" Job 40.20, let alone my lambs. I'm sure our Creator Lord put a capacity for joy in all His creatures for His delight as well as theirs. Actually, I can't vouch for the likes of earthworms, but who knows what underground rave ups they have.

The most unrestrained and abandoned animals I can think of are lambs who everyone knows like to gambol. And in company with all youngsters their favourite play-time is just before dusk. They go around in a gang, chasing chickens, playing tag or King of the Castle, if they have a straw bale or log to use for battlements. They leap up and down in fantastic acrobatic displays, twisting and turning in mid-air. They are heedless of any danger in these gymnastics and I've sometimes had to pick up the pieces after someone has landed awkwardly. The worst fall resulted in a dislocated shoulder and a trip to the vet, to put it back.

If a small lamb has had to be kept indoors for some days, like Mitey Min for example, the little tot has gambolled about with the cat and dog. Our dining room has a wood-suspended floor and often used to resound with the drumming of tiny hooves as the lamb bounded about on all fours. We always knew all was well with the baby if we could hear a tattoo like that.

Ewes are usually too burdened with care to let themselves go like they did as youngsters, but even they can't help joining the lamb gangs occasionally. I've also seen them let their hair down when especially happy. Even if they are really aged they cannot help jumping for joy at the sight of some fresh, new pasture or an especially delicious treat. Then they take their partners for the Sheep Scud; they run in formation in a series of bounding leaps, as all four feet leave the ground. It looks hilarious, particularly when they still bounce up and down on the spot once they've come to a halt – as though they're on pogo sticks.

Since cattle are so much more weighty, if they tried such athletics they'd probably do themselves an injury. But they have a very real sense of fun and the calves, just like the lambs, play in a group, head butting each other, and skittering about, all the while making silly noises. Their mothers also love to have mock battles with the 'enemy' – which may be a pile of straw, a bale of hay or straw or each other.

There's nothing they like better than to push the object all over the place, dancing about as they do. They also adore a 'dust bath' and a 'mud pack' – they find an earthy patch, get on to their knees, rub their faces in it, then paw the soil backwards all over themselves. Others join in this knees-up, and have a frenzied jamboree egged on by the spectators.

But the funniest sight occurred one Spring on the day I let a small group out for the first time in 3 months. (If the winter is very wet cows must be kept off the grass, otherwise they will poach it – no, not like eggs! – they puddle the grass into a quagmire and ruin it.) At that time I didn't have enough land to give them a winter sacrifice field (i.e. the grass is sacrificed to them). So the day had finally arrived when the pasture was long enough and dry enough for the cows to come out. This is always an exciting event and all the cattle have to run about in sheer delight with their tails in the air. But that wasn't enough for Honey. She could barely keep still as I opened their gate, and as her feet touched the grass her whole body quivered. Then she did something I've never seen before or since. She began to dance the Cow Caper (set of course to Moo-d Music!) The step sequence went like this. Two front hooves up, then down; two back feet up, kick out, down. As her rhythm developed she added the most startling variation. All four feet off the ground and bounce (in good sheep fashion). Perhaps she'd been having dancing lessons from the ewes. While she carried on bouncing, the ground began to shake at the half-ton pounding it was getting. And she went on pogo-sticking until she was puffed out. She'd been leaping with pure joy and delight and it was so infectious that even giant Folly tried to join in. But the co-ordination was beyond her - she's probably got four left feet, I fear.

This reminds me of the time David "danced before the Lord with all his might", 2 Sam 6.4. His joy was so full at bringing the Ark of God up to his city, that he wasn't afraid to let himself go and forget he was a King, and just abandon himself to his love and joy in His God. Nor was he bothered about people's reactions. His wife Michal watched and despised him (to her cost) but David wanted to delight in His Lord and have His approval, not his subjects'.

Joying in the Lord rings out throughout the Old Testament, but those who do not know God and the delights of friendship with Him cannot understand all this. God, Christianity, the Bible, are perceived as dull, po-faced and restrictive. They've missed the most exquisite joy and this joy can be ours in Christ Jesus, John 15.11. That ought to be enough to start any of us doing the Sheep Scud or even the Cow Caper.

A WELL 'TO-DO'

There's an ancient iron-wheeled hay turner on the farm which looks as though it dates back to the Romans' occupation. And as far as I'm concerned they can come back and have it! Mike actually used it one summer, behind his equally antique Fergie Tractor, but it now moulders in a

corner. Maybe the Roman legions who were guarding Brancaster Fort (a couple of miles on the coast from here) once used it as a chariot. Then they may have swapped it for some food supplies grown on the Villa, which now lies under one of my fields. And those farmers would probably have felt the same way about it as I do!

We must have quite a lot in common because I know they also kept small, black cattle (like Dexters) and multi-coloured sheep. So they must look down on my activities rather scornfully and think; "Well it's 1,500 years on from our days, and she's no further advanced". (And if they've seen me using flints as knives to cut bailer twine etc...!!) Still, they might be just a tad jealous of my electric fences, and they would be horrified at the greatest difference since their times. This concerns the geography of the valley (now a dry tributary of the River Burn). It is so serious a change that the Romans would never have settled here today.

They always chose well-watered sites for towns or villages and no doubt they found springs as well as a stream in my valley. But now it is as dry as a bone and even in the two decades we've lived at the farm, we have seen drastic water-level falls. When we first came we completely relied on well-water for both the farm and house, since the water main was a mile away in the village. We didn't see a problem in this situation, because the well was 160ft deep and had not even been overly low in the Great Drought of 1975-6. For our first seven years, we had no reason to be worried about the water supply. However, during that time a neighbouring farmer had sunk a new 450 feet-deep bore only 400 metres away from us in the same valley. Despite assurances from the N.R.A., that all would be well (puns could come in here all the time), this bore and the dry years of 1989, 1990, 1991 and 1992 spelt disaster for us.

In the first of those summers our pump burnt out, because unknown to us, it was running dry! A very costly replacement was barely installed before the N.R.A. told us we must stop pumping at once. Our water woes were only just beginning and those Romans must be very glad they missed them. You would be forgiven for not realising how grim this was to be for us and our livestock and the family of 5 we supplied who lived in a near-by property. For 3 years we were to have <u>NO WATER</u> in the houses, unless we physically carried in containers which we had filled from a stand-pipe in the village. To be able to use our heating systems we had to haul these up into our lofts and fill the storage tanks in this way. Very, very occasionally in the three winter months we could sometimes pump enough to fill the house tanks once a day for 10 minutes. So, none of us could bath, or do any washing, and we had to learn to wash in a pint or so we saved from the drinking containers. Kind friends sometimes offered us baths (probably to make us socially acceptable for their dinner parties!) On rare occasions we struggled the 20 miles to the nearest Laundrette and commandeered all the machines! This also continued by the way, through Mike's illness.

However, the house shortages were as nothing compared with the lack of water for the cattle. I'm sure you would not know (unless you farm) that a lactating cow, the size of a Folly or Honey, needs 20-25 gallons a day in the summer. She could almost suck a river dry like Job's Behemoth (Chap. 40). At that time, we had a herd of 50, not all cows, thank goodness, and they needed up to <u>300 gallons a day</u>. Someone suggested that the Water Board would bring out a Bowser to use for them – on enquiring we found it would cost £35.00 a time – i.e about £300 a week!!! So, we had to fetch water from a mains tap, a mile distant, in a Bowser every day, without fail, even when Mike was ill. It took two of us to manage the tackle involved, and was a continual living nightmare.

You may be thinking, "why ever didn't they deepen the well?" – Two simple answers – the cost and the uncertainty of success, remembering the depth of the irrigation bores around. "Well then, what about the Water Board?" Oh! We tried them right at the beginning, but the £30,000 bill was beyond us! It was too uneconomic for them to bring the mains down for just 2 customers. We then tried to get grants and approached anyone who'd take up our case. So for three years letters plied back and forth while the situation got worse and the stress was often almost unbearable.

Then suddenly in the Spring, after Mike's death, everything happened at once. Government and Council aid and our contributions at last added up to the Water Board's satisfaction. Then on the very day that digging began to bring the main pipe-line to us, the N.R.A. set in motion the deepening of the well (since they had agreed that the irrigation extractions had threatened it). And one of the daily readings for that day which I was using had this glorious verse; "He turns the wilderness into a standing water, and the dry ground into water springs", Ps. 107.35. And He certainly had!

At last, the cows were on tap to the well again, and I had mains water and could actually experience the delights of an automatic washing machine, and I could flush the loo once again! I'm afraid the whole experience has made it very difficult for me to sympathise with those who are angry or upset at water restrictions like a hose pipe ban. Everyone expects that there will always be water in their taps; but if they only knew the present state of the acquifers, (water bearing rock layers). They are over 12 feet lower than in 1994 and still falling, and the mains bores of West Norfolk are under threat, let alone my well. 'They' won't be able to supply water if God doesn't send us rain. Man is not in control as he so fondly imagines – he may use irrigation and all modern means, but the climate is in God's hands and not ours, as the drought-hit areas of the Third World know only too well. Twentieth Century technology has almost become a kind of god today, but it cannot overrule the elements any more than my Romans of 400 A.D. were able to do.

Even though it was the 1990's, the cows and sheep along with us humans panted like the deer in Ps. 42, longing for the relief of streams of water during those terrible heat waves. Physically we were all in need, but Mike and I also longed for our God and His aid during those wilderness years (which included our cancers too). Our souls felt the drought just as keenly as our bodies and we needed Isaiah's words of solace in Chap. 50 "Come all of you who are thirsty. Come to the waters you who have no money".

When cows are desperate they have been known to drink anything, even diesel oil with fatal effects. And we humans will 'swig down' almost any ideology that is easy to swallow. But God has implanted a longing for Him in our souls, we were made in God's image – and only He can satisfy. We were made for fellowship and friendship with Him and our souls will never let us forget that. And we don't need to set off with a bowser for that water, it is on permanent tap if we will keep our hearts and lives open to Him.

LIVING FOSSILS

There's a living fossil here on the farm (No! it's not me!) It's a rather unprepossessing tree, which is to be found in my garden. Even though it was planted 15 years ago, it's still only 10' tall and sparse with it. Mind you, it has had to fight back, year after year from attacks by passing sheep who can't seem to resist it. Wherever we have

lived, Michael planted one of these trees because its origin fascinated him. His interest in horticulture and gardening was deep and informed and he loved attending open-days at parks, gardens or arboretums. On a visit to one of the latter, once we had moved here, he found himself being proudly shown a sickly-looking specimen that he instantly recognised. The guide then rather importantly addressed the group of visitors: "Does anyone know what kind of tree we have here?"

There was a stunned silence. "Yes", piped up Mike, "it's a Metasequoia Glyptostroboides and I've got one at home that's twice the size!"

This rather spoilt what was to have been the climax of that day's tour. The tree is usually accorded a reverence due only to Archbishops! So what has the Metasequoia Glyptostroboides got, apart from an almost unpronounceable and un-spellable name? What is it that draws farmers, gardeners, tree experts and sheep to its feet in awe?

Is it because it is a <u>deciduous</u> conifer? Is it the weird bark and strange leaf/needle formation?

Is it because it is tasty? (Only a sheep can answer that one.) No, I would suggest it's none of these. It is the fact that it is a prehistoric tree and I'll quote from Creation Magazine June 1997: "It seems that the psychological appeal of having a prehistoric tree in your back yard over-rides simple logic".

That was actually being said about another living fossil, the Wollemi Pine found growing in the National Park near Sydney,

Australia. Until 1994, it had only been known from identical fossils in 'so-called' dinosaur age rock. Now 500 specimens have been produced from seeds and cuttings to meet a public demand. (And I know someone who would have snapped one up!)

The Metasequoia Glyptostroboides was found in China in 1947, and had only previously been known by fossil remains. And again seeds were germinated in both the U.K and U.S.A. to make sure plenty of people would have something to boast about!

Of course, for those of us who are hooked on animal fossils, these discoveries are old hat. We've known for some time that there are literally hundreds of creatures which are identical in fossil and living form. So fossils are alive and well and all over the place and haven't evolved one tiny bit. Man may have developed domestic animals like the cow or sheep, but they are essentially the same as the fossils found in fossil graveyards, as for example in the Siwalik Hills north of Delhi.

"Indeed the overwhelming message of the fossil record is one of staying the same not evolving" – states Joachim Scheven on the video "Living Fossils",

Well, neither my cattle nor ewes (nor my neighbours' pigs) know all this but they do know that they produce babies which are exactly like them – i.e. – "after/according to their kind: Genesis 1.24 etc. No matter what breeding programmes I introduced, I could not evolve a lamb into calf; although I should get variations in size and colour, shape, and I certainly have! Dog breeders have also seen many developments, but these are not evolution as essentially meant by Darwinists. A Papillon and a Great Dane are both dogs, with a leg at each corner, and have still bred "after their kind".

And no 'missing links' have ever been found, no matter what rumours we hear: - Darwin 100 years ago doubted any ever would be, and so it has proved. So much that is presented as fact, on our T.V.'s etc. is just man's ideas and hopes, especially as man's mind is naturally hostile to God and he prefers to believe in a lie. Romans 1.18-25.

But back to fossils – the very word has come to mean **OLD**; but many fossils are **ALIVE AND WELL** as we've seen. And those fossils of stone are not as 'old' as we are led to believe. First and foremost fossil dating is totally unreliable. The confident assertions about the age of some dinosaur find for example, are **UNPROVED** (in fact, recent finds of blood cells and D.N.A. in dinosaur remains means that these are **YOUNG** – less than 10,000 years because otherwise these materials would have decayed). This is very embarrassing for evolutionists as they claim dinosaurs died out 60 million years ago!

Fossils need rapid burial to remain intact – for example in 1878 miners found 39 complete Iguanodon skeletons of dinosaurs in a coal seem. Each 10 metres long, several metres high and weighing 2 tons apiece – only very fast burial in tons of sediment would have left them undamaged. Many fossils show such detail of eyes, or skin, or actually have their original organic ligaments, that the creature was buried within hours and had no time to deteriorate. Fossils are found in deep, deep layers of sediment (water deposits) all over the world, all jumbled up with so called 'primitive, ancient' forms lying beside 'recent' ones – i.e. they lived and died together. With traces of D.N.A. etc. in them, pointing to a catastrophe occurring less than 10,000 years to bring about their mass destruction. Isn't there a bit about that in God's Word?!! Genesis Chapter 6-8, and Jesus referred to it as fact – "a global flood of judgement". Do we believe and trust in Jesus Christ? Then we have to believe what He believed (rather, knew, of course).

My living fossils (and I suppose I am one too!) and my fossil collection uphold God's truth and revelation of Creation and Flood which we find in Genesis, but which is also such a part and parcel of the Bible account and letters and prophesies, that if we cut them all out, we wouldn't have much left. Whether I am looking at Honey or Steel or holding a trilobite fossil, I can see the glory of my Creator Father, whose designer skills are breathtaking. D.N.A., life's building-block, is in everything, with a different programme for a tree or sheep or me. Same D.N.A., but a new code - sounds simple but your code can fill more than an Encyclopaedia Britannica! And your code is unique to you (or to me) so there can never be another Jenny Sparks (thank goodness for that!!) and never another Steel Sparks. His D.N.A. code said: "Make an Alsatian Dog – Make a Unique Alsatian Dog – i.e. Steel". So we are all made in loving care and detail - we are uniquely precious to Him. This knowledge is almost too much to take in – what a Creator God is ours! "We are fearfully and wonderfully made," Psalm 139.4. David wrote that without the benefit of our information – how much more praise he would have given His Maker if he'd had such data.

And David didn't stop at praise, he loved his Lord, Psalm 18.1. "I love you, O Lord", for he knew His mighty Creator "reached down from on high and took hold of me... rescued me" Psalm 18.16. Why does God love us? A verse in Deut. 7.7,8, gives us our answer "Our God did not set His love upon us or choose us for anything in us,...

but because the Lord loved us". No other reason, but because He loved us.

I am often asked by friends why I stay at the farm and do all the hard labour – surely I must be quite dotty. Maybe, but I do so because I love the cattle and sheep. However, anyone seeing them would say - "But they're just a motley crew, no animal looks especially worth your care; let's face it, you haven't got any amazing pedigree paragons".

That's quite correct; but I know them as individuals, each unique in their way, with their own eccentricities. And I love each one, just because I know and love them. And only I know the great joy and delight they give me, especially in their response and their love given to me in return.

Our Father, God loves us like that and we can rejoice His heart, by loving Him with all our hearts and minds and strength and living to His Glory. What a thought! You and I can make Our Creator God delighted and pleased.

"May the Lord rejoice in His Works", Psalm 104.31, when He looks at each one of us.